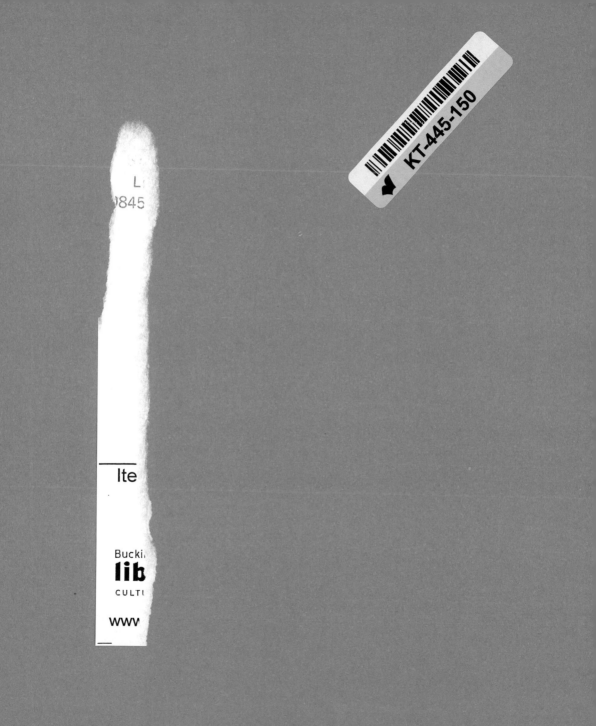

KT-445-150

L
0845

Ite

Bucki
lib
CULTI

www

# Puppy Training and Care

TRACY LIBBY

Project Team
Editor: Heather Russell-Revesz
Copy Editor: Joann Woy
Indexer: Elizabeth Walker
Interior Design: Leah Lococo Ltd. and Stephanie Krautheim
Design Layout: Stephanie Krautheim

First published in the United Kingdom 2009 by

Interpet Publishing

Vincent Lane

Dorking

Surrey

RH4 3YX

ISBN 978 1 84286 207 0

United Kingdom Editorial Team

Claire Cullinan

Hannah Turner

Nicola Parker

| Buckinghamshire County Council | | |
| --- | --- | --- |
| 2640277 | | |
| Askews | | Nov-2009 |
| 636.70887 | | £10.99 |
| | | |

©2008 T.F.H. Publications, Inc.

All rights reserved. No part of this publication may be reproduced, stored, or transmitted in any form, or by any means electronic, mechanical or otherwise, without written permission from Interpet Publishing, except where permitted by law. Requests for permission or further information should be directed to the above address.

Printed and bound in China

This book has been published with the intent to provide accurate and authoritative information in regard to the subject matter within. While every reasonable precaution has been taken in preparation of this book, the author and publisher expressly disclaim responsibility for any errors, omissions, or adverse effects arising from the use or application of the information contained herein. The techniques and suggestions are used at the reader's discretion and are not to be considered a substitute for veterinary care. If you suspect a medical problem consult your veterinarian.

Promoting responsible pet ownership

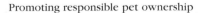

**INTERPET**
PUBLISHING

www.interpet.co.uk

# Table of Contents

# Chapter 1

# Ready for Me?

# Puppy Prepping

Acquiring a puppy is an enormous responsibility because he will be depending on you for all of his basic needs, including food, grooming, training, and love! You'll also have to be careful to never put him in a position where he can get himself into trouble. That's why puppy-proofing your home before your new four-legged friend arrives is of utmost importance.

## Puppy Proof

Just as you kid-proof your house for babies and toddlers, you must puppy-proof your home, too—ideally *before* your precious pooch arrives. Puppies, like toddlers, love to explore their surroundings and will try to put everything in their mouth—whether it fits or not. Puppies love to chew, and they cannot distinguish between an inexpensive chew toy and an expensive leather purse. Pick up anything and everything your puppy is likely to seek out and destroy, including electrical cables, books, newspapers, decorative cushions, shoes, purses, dolls, houseplants, and so forth.

## Don't Forget the Outside

Puppy-proof your garage and garden areas by picking up garden hoses, sprinklers, and garden ornaments. Fence off any garden areas your puppy is likely to destroy, such as prized rose or vegetable gardens. Store containers of poisonous products—fertilisers, herbicides, pesticides, and the like—on shelves and out of reach of inquisitive puppies.

Puppies can be master escape artists, too. Walk around your property, making sure your fences are secure, with no holes, missing boards, or broken gates that he is likely to escape through. Is the height of your fence sufficient to contain a Pomeranian? Shetland Sheepdog? Rottweiler? If your garden is unfenced, consider fencing it or at least fence a portion of the garden where

your puppy can be safely confined for short periods. Otherwise, be sure your puppy is on lead each and every time he goes outdoors. Your job is to keep him safe. He does not have the mental wherewithal to understand that the street is a dangerous place to be.

## What to Buy

Now that you've puppy-proofed your house, here's the really exciting part—shopping! From pet shops and canine boutiques to catalogues and online vendors, you can literally shop 'till you drop! Be savvy and shop around, but don't sacrifice quality for cost. Remember, cost doesn't always equate to quality and, when possible, it is always prudent to invest in good-quality, top-notch products.

## Bed

Your puppy will need a comfy bed to call his own. A place to rest his head, not to mention his weary bones, after a fun-filled day of playing, training,

*To keep your puppy safe, puppy-proof both the inside and outside of your home.*

and all that goes into being a puppy! However, prudence dictates holding off on the expensive designer model until your puppy is well through the chewing stage. Puppies chew. It's a fact of life. Some breeds are more tenacious than others, and countless stories have been told of puppies shredding expensive beds in the few minutes it takes their owner to shower, take out the rubbish, or answer the telephone.

A large blanket or towel folded over several times, or a cosy fleece pad placed in his crate or exercise pen will do the job for the first few months.

Once your puppy is through the chewing stage, choose a size-appropriate bed. To save on cost, purchase one that will be large enough for your puppy as he grows—especially if you have acquired one of the large breeds. Available in a variety of material, colours, shapes, and sizes, dog beds are frequently filled with down, cotton, poly blends, or memory foam. Others are filled with material for odour and insect control. Choose a bed that has a removable fleece or cotton cover that is easily cleaned in the washing machine.

## Collar

Collars serve an important function, and you should never sacrifice quality and comfort for style. But that doesn't mean you can't indulge your own sense of style when choosing one—or two! Collars come in a variety of materials— the most popular being leather and

### How Does Your Garden Grow?

**Avoid using poisonous products in your garden and on your lawn several weeks before your puppy arrives, so that he isn't digging in soil or playing on grass that has been treated with poisonous chemicals. If possible, avoid using them altogether once your new puppy arrives. A number of natural and/or nonpoisonous products are available for use around dogs, cats, and other animals.**

nylon. Nylon is relatively inexpensive and available in every colour of the rainbow, with countless designs. Braided, rolled, or flat leather collars are more expensive, but well worth the investment for adult dogs because they are long-lasting and comfortable.

Puppies grow quickly, so check his collar regularly to ensure a proper fit, replacing it as he grows bigger and stronger.

## Crate

One of the more expensive items on your must-have list is a crate. This is where your puppy will sleep and where he will be confined for short periods when you cannot watch him like a hawk, such as when you jump in the shower. It should be in place before you bring your puppy home,

7

Ready for Me? Puppy Prepping

because you want him to associate it with his new home and all things good in his life, such as eating, sleeping, and retreating from the poking, prodding fingers of toddlers and the often chaotic and noisy world of humans. Crates are also ideal for travelling and housetraining.

## What Size?

Purchase a crate that is big enough for your puppy when he is full grown. Ideally, it should be big enough so that, when your puppy is full grown, he has enough room to stand up, turn around, and stretch out while lying down. If the crate is too big, it defeats the purpose of providing the security of a den. During the housetraining stage, a crate that is too large allows a puppy to use one end for sleeping and the other end as a bathroom, which defeats its usefulness as a housetraining tool. However, if it is too small, your dog will be cramped and uncomfortable, and this is neither fair nor humane. Some crates come equipped with a divider panel that allows you to adjust the crate space accordingly. This type of crate can take your dog from the puppy stage through housetraining and into adulthood.

## What Type?

Crates come in a variety of materials, and each offers its own advantages. Folding wire crates are easy to transport between house and car and provide good air circulation, keeping your pooch cool when temperatures are high. They also provide good

# FAMILY-FRIENDLY TIP

## Kid Chores

Here are some ways in which your child can be included in day-to-day doggie chores:

- Make a contract with her about her canine responsibilities and chores.
- Post a rota or chores chart for your child outlining the puppy's feeding and potty times. Have her sound the alarm at the designated chore times, and check off each chore as it's completed.
- Designate a daily 10-minute grooming session, and put your child in charge of the grooming tools including brush, comb, doggie toothbrush, and toothpaste.
- Let your child be in charge of the food bowl. It will be her job to get it out, fill it, clean it, and put it away.
- Put your child in charge of emptying, cleaning, and refilling Fido's water bowl at least twice a day.
- Pay a cash bonus for any child who picks up a dog mess.

visibility for your dog and, at a glance, you will be able to keep tabs on him.

Other types include heavy-duty high-impact plastic kennels that meet requirements for airline travel. Nylon crates are lightweight and portable, but they may not be the ideal choice for the tenacious chewer.

A good quality crate will last a lifetime, and the benefits definitely make it well worth the cost when one considers the alternative of replacing damaged carpet and furniture six months down the road.

## Food and Water Bowls

Mealtimes are some of your puppy's favourite times, and no doubt they will remain so as he grows bigger and stronger. From custom-painted ceramic ware to stainless steel to durable plastic bowls, the selection is seemingly endless, and that means your precious pooch can always dine in style! Be sure your puppy has bowls for both food and water.

You'll also want to purchase size-appropriate bowls. What works for a Chihuahua will be too small for a Dalmatian and vice versa. Some bowls are designed with small openings that help long-eared breeds keep their ears outside the bowl. You also can purchase special bowl stands that raise the bowls up off the ground.

- **Stainless Steel:** Ideally, you should focus on stainless steel because it's durable, virtually indestructible, easily sanitised and—perhaps the most important—dishwasher safe. Some bowls come with rubber bases to keep dogs from pushing them around on the floor.

- **Plastic:** Plastic bowls are inexpensive, but they are not the best choice for the tenacious chewer, who might ingest or choke on shredded pieces. Also, plastic is not as easily sanitised as stainless steel and can harbour bacteria.

- **Ceramic:** Ceramic bowls are stylish and decorative, but they are breakable and usually expensive. If you choose this route, be sure

*A crate is very useful when housetraining your puppy.*

*Stainless steel is a good choice for your puppy's food and water bowls.*

that the ceramic is finished with a nontoxic glaze and is dishwasher safe.

## Grooming Tools

Grooming tools are an absolute necessity and, while purchasing top-notch equipment is more expensive, in the long run it is less expensive than repeatedly replacing inferior equipment.

Even if you plan to have your puppy professionally groomed, you will want to have on hand a few essential items for general grooming including a brush or two, nail clippers, ear cleaner, toothbrush, doggie toothpaste, and shampoo made for dogs. You might consider a grooming table, too. While initially expensive to purchase, they make grooming a lot easier for you and more enjoyable for your dog.

## Identification

No one likes to think of losing their precious pooch but, despite your best efforts, accidents do happen. It's possible that you and your puppy may become separated. The best way to stack the odds in favour of his returning home safely is identification. Two common types of identification are ID tags and microchips. Ideally, your puppy should have both.

### ID Tags

Be sure that your puppy always wears a buckle collar with an identification tag that includes, at the minimum, your name and telephone number.

Available in a variety of shapes, sizes, colours, and materials, they easily attach to your puppy's buckle collar with an S-clip or split ring. Some ID tags attach directly to the collar, not unlike a nameplate on a horse's halter. Unfortunately, tags aren't 100 percent dependable. Tags can fall off a dog's collar. They can rust, fade, or get scratched, making the engraving difficult, if not impossible to read. Collars can break or slip off and, if your dog isn't wearing his collar, the tag will be of no use.

### Microchips

Microchips offer a permanent method of identification because they cannot be lost, altered, or intentionally removed. A microchip is a tiny computer chip—about the size of a grain of rice—that has an identification number programmed into it. The chip is painlessly and permanently inserted under your puppy's skin, usually between the shoulder blades, by a veterinarian. Once a puppy or adult dog is "chipped," this one-of-a-kind identification number can identify him throughout his life. The identification number is recorded on a central database along with your name, address, and telephone number.

If your wayward dog turns up at a veterinarian's surgery or rescue centre, his microchip can be scanned and, within mere seconds, his identification number will pop up on the hand-held scanner. The ID number is then cross-referenced with your contact information via a registry.

## Dog Duty

Your puppy can't take care of himself, so he is depending on you for food, water, training, exercise, grooming, veterinary care, hugs, kisses, and unconditional love. To ensure his needs are met on a regular daily basis, post a schedule and choose appropriate family members to help out.

## Lead

You should have no problem indulging your own sense of style when it comes to choosing a lead and, when all is said and done, choosing a lead is really a matter of preference. However, don't forget they serve an important function. Never sacrifice style for comfort, quality, and durability.

### Nylon

Nylon leads are lightweight and relatively inexpensive, which means you can afford to stock up, keeping an extra one around the house or in your car. Available in a variety of colours and designs, they work great for puppies and small breeds. However, they are not always the best choice for strong dogs because they are hard on your hands and can slice your fingers to the bone should a big dog give a good lunge or pull.

### Leather

Leather leads are more expensive than nylon but well worth the investment because they are softer on your hands. That's a good thing because you'll be using your lead a lot, and the more you use it the more soft and pliable it becomes. Leather leads come in a variety of shapes—flat, rolled, or braided—as well as in different sizes—both width and length. The key to avoiding costly mistakes is to buy a size-appropriate lead for your dog that will fit him when he is full grown. Imagine trying to control a 200-pound (91 kg) St. Bernard on a 3/8-inch (.9 cm) lead that is more suitable for a

10-pound (5 kg) Miniature Pinscher. Most small-breed dogs will do quite well with a 1/2- or 5/8-inch (1.3- or 1.6-cm) wide leather lead. Medium dogs will benefit from a 5/8- or 3/4-inch (1.6- or 1.9-cm) wide lead, and large breeds may require a 1-inch (2.5-cm) wide lead.

Most large or strong breed puppies, such as Staffordshire Bull Terriers, Rottweilers, Great Danes, and so forth, will do just fine on a heavier lead (i.e., 3/4- or 1-inch [2- to 2.5-cm] wide lead) because, even as puppies, they are generally quite strong and/or large. Also, the puppies of large and/or strong breeds grow quite quickly and, even if you do not need a heavier lead when he is ten weeks old, you will need it within a month or two. If money is no option, you may decide to purchase a lightweight lead for his first few months and a size-appropriate lead for when he enters his junior and adult years.

### Harnesses

Depending on the breed you have acquired, a harness may be a viable option. It will not keep your dog from pulling, but it will take the pressure off his trachea, because the harness goes around his body, not his neck. A variety of models are available in different shapes, sizes, and materials. Seek professional advice to fit your dog correctly with a harness and prevent chafing.

### Toys

You can never have too many toys when you own a puppy! They should be at the top of your absolutely-must-have list because dogs love to chew, and they need to chew—especially puppies, who will experience teething as their baby teeth erupt and fall out, and again when their adult teeth come in. Chewing helps to relieve the pain and irritation of teething, and that's why it's important you have plenty of suitable chew toys. Otherwise, your puppy will find other things to chew on—and that normally includes your designer shoes, purses, decorative cushions, table legs, and so forth.

It's important to choose age- and size-appropriate chew toys. The healthiest and most long-lasting chew toys will be toys made for your breed's body type and chewing style. For example, chew toys designed for a Yorkshire Terrier are too small for a Staffordshire

*A harness takes the pressure off your puppy's neck.*

## Retractable Leads

Designed to extend and retract at the touch of a button, a retractable lead allows your puppy plenty of distance on walks without carrying a long line that can get tangled, dragged through the mud, or wrapped around bushes. Retractable leads come in different sizes and retractable lengths. The key is selecting a size-appropriate lead. A mini-retractable lead that extends 10 feet (3 m) and works wonders on an 8-pound (4 kg) Italian Greyhound will be useless for a 150-pound (63 kg) Mastiff—and vice versa.

Bull Terrier and could present a choking hazard.

Always choose toys that are safe and not likely to break into pieces and cause choking hazards.

For real gnawing and gnashing, choose toys that are strong, durable, and well made, such as hard nylon and rubber toys. They exercise your dog's teeth, gums, and jaws, promoting oral health while relieving the need to chew.

Adorable squeaky toys are usually irresistible, but may not be the best selection for the tenacious chewer. A determined puppy (or adult dog) will chew right through the material and may swallow the stuffing or squeaker, which could become lodged in his throat or intestines.

If your puppy has access to all his toys, all the time, he'll lose interest in them. Stash a few toys, and then surprise him with a new one when he least expects it. Save his favourite toys in reserve, such as a flying disc or rope tug, for special interactive occasions.

## X-pens and Baby Gates

Exercise pens and baby gates corral curious puppies, keep them away from household hazards, and prevent them from developing bad habits, such as peeing from one end of the house to the other, chewing furniture, and ransacking rubbish bins. Exercise pens, or X-pens, as they are often called, are ideal anywhere you need a temporary kennel area, such as in the kitchen, family room, or back garden.

When strategically placed, baby gates give your puppy (or adult dog) a bit more freedom indoors without allowing him free run of the house. Just like baby gates for toddlers, they easily attach to door frames, confining your dog to one room or part of the house.

# Chapter 2

# Welcome Home!

You have been eagerly awaiting your puppy's arrival, and the big day has finally arrived. Your home is a whole new world for him and for the first few days, your puppy may be frightened and uncertain, which is only natural. It is your job to provide a safe and secure environment and love him unconditionally for the next 10 to 15 years.

## Collecting Your Puppy

Perhaps you are lucky enough to have your puppy delivered to your doorstep. Most likely, however, you will need to pick him up. Doing so isn't terribly difficult, but it does require a bit of planning. Most well-bred, well-socialised puppies from reputable breeders will have few difficulties adjusting to their new home, provided a few precautions are in place.

Ideally, your puppy should ride in his crate. With any luck, the crate training process will have been started and your puppy will feel safe and secure. Resist the urge to allow your puppy to ride on your lap or wander around the vehicle. A nervous or distressed puppy may vomit or try to squirm out of your arms. A loose puppy runs the risk of falling or injuring himself. There will be plenty of time for cuddles and kisses when you get home.

Keep noises and distractions to a minimum, too. This includes kids squealing, hollering, and poking tiny fingers into the puppy's crate. The transition to your home should be calm and positive.

Keep stomach upsets to a minimum by purchasing bottled water. After a few days, you can start mixing in your own water, or continue using bottled water.

For the same reason, ask the breeder to send home about a week's worth of your puppy's food. Avoid changing his diet for the first few days. If he's eating a good-quality puppy food, consider continuing with the same diet. If you plan to switch foods, do so a few days after your puppy has settled in, and introduce the new diet gradually over a 7 to 10 day period.

## Your Puppy's New Home

Upon arriving home, allow your puppy plenty of time to urinate outdoors before taking him indoors. Be sure to

*Set your puppy up for success, and soon he'll be right at home!*

## Comfort Cloth

Some breeders place an old towel or T-shirt in with the puppies, which absorbs the scent of his canine mother and littermates. The breeder sends this scented "comfort cloth" home in the puppy's crate. For the first few nights, your puppy may find this reassuring and comforting because it smells familiar.

stay with him. Leaving him unattended in a strange garden may add to any existing nervousness or distress. Equally important, staying with him allows you to supervise his activity and be sure he has emptied his bladder and bowels.

Once indoors, keep him sequestered in one area, such as the kitchen, family room, or living room, where you can watch him like a hawk. Never, never, never give him free run of the house at this age, because you will be putting him in a position to develop bad habits, such as peeing from one end of the house to the other.

You will also want to start right away establishing a daily routine. Feed your puppy at the same time each day,

and remember to take him outdoors regularly to facilitate housetraining and prevent accidents. (See Chapter 6 for more on housetraining).

## Introducing Children

Introducing your puppy to your children and other pets in the house is relatively straightforward. Keep in mind that, unless your puppy was raised around children at the breeder's house, your puppy may not be accustomed to the activity, noise, and quick movements of children. Take care to introduce both puppy and children in a quiet, nonstressful environment, keeping the pandemonium to a minimum so as not to startle, overwhelm, or frighten your puppy. Even a bold and confident puppy will likely be stressed and overwhelmed by noisy, rambunctious children running wildly, flailing their arms, or roughhousing.

After a few days, when your puppy has settled into his new home, he should become accustomed to the litany of chaos associated with raising children.

Most good-natured puppies do quite well in a household when they are raised with children, established guidelines are followed, and children are clearly supervised. Supervision is the key to preventing injuries, instilling appropriate behaviours, and discouraging unwanted behaviours—in both puppies and children. Most children under the age of 7 do not understand the consequences of their actions. They see nothing wrong with

# Setting Up a Schedule

For the first few months, your puppy's schedule will be to wake up, potty, play, eat, potty, play, potty, sleep, wake up, potty, eat lunch, potty, play, potty, sleep, wake up, potty, play, potty, eat dinner, potty, play, potty, play, potty, sleep, wake up, potty, play, potty, sleep. Of course, in between all the toileting, eating, and playing, you'll want to incorporate several short, fun training sessions, as well as a lot socialisation—rides in the car, and trips to the veterinarian, bank, dry cleaners, and so forth.

Dogs are creatures of habit, learning through repetition and consistency. The more consistent you are with his schedule, the quicker he will adjust to living in your household. If necessary, jot down a schedule and post it in a conspicuous spot so that your puppy is not overlooked or forgotten. Have the kids sound the alarm at the appropriate feeding and toileting times, and have them check it off the list when completed.

If you work during the day, confine your puppy in an exercise pen and have a trusted friend, neighbour, or relative come by several times to potty and exercise him. You may also want to consider enlisting the help of a professional dog walker who can stop by several times a day to exercise and potty your puppy. That said, it is worth mentioning that your puppy is extremely impressionable during the first 8 to 20 weeks of his life. If you go this route, be sure your puppy is learning good and positive behaviours and not being subjected to fearful or inappropriate behaviours, such as roughhousing, verbal or physical abuse, and so forth.

Be sure to give him plenty of exercise before you leave for work. This will help to tire him out a bit. And don't forget plenty of toys and a yummy bone or chew toy to keep him occupied for a few hours.

trying to pick up a puppy by his ears or clutching him for dear life. They do not understand that they can seriously injure a puppy or young dog if they pick up him up incorrectly or drop him.

At the other end of the spectrum, when a puppy is allowed to play unsupervised with several young children, you end up with an adult dog who has learned to chase, jump, and nip at arms and legs in motion.

## Introducing Other Dogs

Introducing your puppy to other animals in the house can be a bit tricky, but with some organisation and a bit of planning things can go smoothly. The key is supervision and never allowing other pets to intimidate or overwhelm your puppy—or vice versa.

Introduce your other dog (or dogs) in a controlled and stress-free environment, such as the living room or back garden. Stay close, but avoid interfering unless the older dog becomes too pushy or bossy—or vice versa. Puppies can easily be injured should they be pawed, rolled, or stepped on by bigger dogs. Keep a close eye on both puppy and adult dog to avoid any problems. Keep introductions brief, fun, and positive to avoid overwhelming either animal. Gradually increase the amount of supervised time they spend together until both animals appear to be comfortable.

Puppies also have a lot more energy than senior dogs, so never allow your puppy to harass, antagonise, or bother your older dog when he is sleeping, resting, or eating.

19

*Supervise all interactions between your puppy and child.*

How quickly your dog takes to adjust and accept a new puppy will depend on the temperament and character of your adult dog. Some dogs are happy-go-lucky and will readily accept any newcomers. Other dogs are more set in their ways and less willing to share their owners' attention and affection.

Older dogs are often, albeit inadvertently, neglected in the presence of a new puppy. Be sure to give as much attention and affection to your older dog as he received before the new puppy arrived. Avoid disrupting the older dog's routine too much, and remind him regularly that he is still an important and valuable member of the family.

## Introducing Cats

Despite the old adage, "Fighting like cats and dogs"—cats and dogs can and do live together quite harmoniously.

Introductions between young puppies and cats generally go quite smoothly. Again, the key is to set ground rules from day one. Think ahead to what behaviours you will and will not accept. If you do not want your puppy growing into an adult dog who chases, harasses, and pounces on the cat, do not put him in a position where he can develop bad habits.

To expedite the introduction process, hold your puppy—not the cat. Your cat may hiss and spit at your puppy, which is natural behaviour for cats. Provide your cat plenty of access and opportunity to flee to higher ground, be it furniture or a worktop. If your cat runs, your puppy will most likely give chase. Puppies from the herding group—Australian Shepherds, Border Collies, German Shepherds, and so forth—are notorious for "herding" or chasing cats, as well as other animals, be they horses, goats, or sheep. A lead or long-line will help prevent this behaviour. Simply attach a lead or long-line to your puppy's collar, which he drags around the house. If you notice him preparing to chase the cat, quickly stand on the lead to prevent him from continuing to do so. Lure

*Watch the initial meeting, and don't allow your puppy to be intimidated.*

## Helping Out

**Children—especially the young ones—are always willing to help out. Maximise their eagerness while building a strong human/canine relationship by having children deliver all the things your puppy loves, such as his food, treats, toys, and his lead. Your puppy will quickly learn that good things happen when kids are around.**

him back to you with a fun toy, then play an interactive game, such as a quick retrieve up and down the hall or a game of tug. It won't be long before your puppy realises the cat is not his personal toy for chasing and harassing. Equally important, he will learn that you are his primary source of fun and games.

## House Rules

Establish household rules from day one, and your life will be much easier. Of course, you'll need to make sure everyone in the house is following the same rules. Your children's ages will dictate how much responsibility you give them. These are a few rules you might want to consider.

- Teach children—yours and visitors—to let sleeping dogs lie. Leave the puppy alone when he is sleeping or resting.

- Teach children how to properly pick up a puppy, but establish the rule that they are not to pick up the puppy without supervision. Despite a child's good intentions, a puppy can easily be injured should he be suspended in an awkward position or, heaven forbid, dropped.

- No roughhousing, running wildly, or playing sic 'em games with the puppy. Puppies who are encouraged and allowed to chase and nip will find chasing and nipping delightful games when they are adult dogs.

- No smacking or hitting your puppy (or adult dog). This is neither fair nor humane and can startle, frighten, or anger your puppy. He may grow to fear you and possibly react by biting.

- No tormenting or teasing the puppy by pulling his ears or tail, poking fingers in his eyes, banging pots on his head, or blowing in his face.

- People food is not good for your puppy's health or waistline. It may cause diarrhoea or upset stomach—or both. He should eat his food and his special treats. Puppies who are fed people food quickly learn to beg, which is a difficult habit to break later in life.

- If you do not want your adult dog on the furniture, do not allow the behaviour as a puppy.

- Puppies love to chew. Put away personal items—backpacks, sweaters, shoes, toys—where he cannot reach them.
- Don't allow children to force themselves on your puppy. Puppies tire quickly, and they need their rest and space.

## Puppy's First Night

Your puppy's first few nights will no doubt be stressful for both you and your puppy. Options vary on how you should handle this situation. Ideally, you should place him in his crate next to your bed. With any luck, he will be tired from his big day travelling, exploring his new surroundings, playing, and all that goes into being a puppy. Hopefully, he will sleep through the night. Otherwise, you will need to get up with him if he needs to relieve himself in the middle of the night or early morning.

Chances are high that he may whine or cry when he's first put in his crate. This is to be expected. Never relegate him to the isolation of the utility room, garage, or back garden. Remember, this is his first night away from his doggie mom and littermates. Try putting his "comfort" cloth (if you brought one home from the breeder) or an old towel or T-shirt with your scent on it in his crate. Or give him a yummy chew toy.

Avoid responding to his noisy behaviour—provided, of course, you are certain he does not need to relieve himself. Depending on your puppy's character and personality, he may whine and whimper for few minutes

*Hopefully, your puppy will be tired from his big day in his new home!*

or an hour—or more! He may cry off and on all night and into the early morning. If you respond with soothing or cooing sounds, such as, "It's okay, honey. Mommy loves you," you will inadvertently be reinforcing the noisy behaviour, which can create all sorts of problems down the road. Equally important, never lose your temper and scold or holler at your puppy. By toughing it out the first few nights and ignoring his pitiful pleas, you will help him quickly adjust to sleeping in his crate.

Resist the urge to take him out of his crate and into your bed; while this might stop the whining, your puppy will quickly learn that whining gets him what he wants. Remember, he's not housetrained, either. If you go this route, don't be surprised if you wake up to an unexpected mess. Equally important, think ahead to the behaviours you want your puppy to possess as an adult dog. If you do not want your 110-pound (50 kg) Rottweiler hogging the bed, it is unfair to allow the behaviour when he is a puppy and then scold him when he is an adult and jumps on the bed.

Remember, puppies have little or no bladder control until they are about six months old. If he whimpers and cries

*The Expert Knows*

## What to Do at Night

If your puppy wakes you up when he has to potty, and you find you simply cannot get up several times during the night—cover an area of the floor with newspaper. Kitchens are ideal because they usually have vinyl or tile floors. Set up an exercise pen on top of the newspaper and put his crate inside the exercise pen. At night, leave his crate door open. He will have access to his crate for sleeping, and he can also potty on the paper if he needs to go. The exercise pen will keep him confined to a small area.

This technique works in a pinch. However, it is always worthwhile to make the effort to get up with you puppy if he needs to relieve himself, because teaching your puppy to urinate indoors on newspaper creates its own set of problems.

in the middle of the night, it's a good indication he needs to relieve himself. Get up and take him quickly outside to potty. Yes—even if it's 3 A.M. And snowing! Do not make a fuss or play with him. Let him potty, and calmly praise him, "Good pee, honey." Put him back in his box—with as little fanfare or commotion as possible—until you are ready to get up.

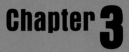

# Feed Me!

Feeding time is no doubt one of your puppy's favourite times! While most puppies will eat anything and everything put in front of them, you will want to provide him with the necessary nutrients to live a healthy, happy life by feeding a complete and balanced diet designed specifically for puppies.

## The Basics

Dogs, like humans, have different nutritional requirements. Puppies, for example, have gigantic nutritional demands, requiring about twice as many calories per pound of body weight as an adult dog of the same breed. Their bodies grow rapidly and, for a puppy's system to build strong muscles, bones, and vital organs, and establish a resistance to disease, he needs a well-balanced, good-quality diet designed specifically for puppies. Puppies also spend a significant part of their day running, jumping, twisting, playing, and everything else that goes into being a puppy—all of which require a lot of calories.

## Feeding by Breed

Some puppies, depending on their breed, may benefit from specially designed foods. For example, large- or giant-breed puppies, such as Rottweilers, Great Danes, or Mastiffs, may benefit from a diet lower in protein, and here's why: In the past,

all puppies were fed the same food regardless of their breed. However, many experts believe that feeding large- and giant-breed puppies a diet lower in protein and fat may reduce the incidence of bone and joint problems that can plague larger breeds. The theory is that, when large- and giant-breed dogs consume too much fat and protein, they grow too quickly, resulting in skeletal abnormalities.

On the other end of the spectrum, small-breed puppies—generally those under 20 pounds (9 kg) when full grown—may benefit from foods with concentrated nutrients specifically designed to meet the nutritional needs of small breeds.

Brachycephalic breeds—breeds that have "pushed-in faces"—can have difficulty eating large kibble-type foods, and may benefit from a smaller food designed specifically for their mouths.

When in doubt, always seek veterinary guidance when choosing or switching puppy foods.

## Nutrition Know-How

Known as *life stage nutrition*, your puppy's unique nutritional requirements are likely to change several times over the course of his life—especially as he grows into an adult dog and then again as he enters his senior years. Despite his changing nutritional needs, the nuts and bolts of canine nutrition remain the same. There

*Think about your breed's needs—a Pug's facial structure may require smaller kibble.*

## Switching Foods

Ideally, for the first few days after bringing your precious pooch home, you should continue feeding the same type and brand of puppy food—provided he has been eating a well-balanced, good-quality puppy food. Of course, depending on where and from whom you purchased your puppy, this may or may not be the case.

If you intend to switch foods, do so slowly—over the course of 7 to 10 days—to prevent intestinal upset, vomiting, constipation, or diarrhoea. To do this, make a mixture of 75 percent old food and 25 percent new food. Feed this mixture for three or four days. Then make a mixture of 50 percent old food and 50 percent new food. Feed this mixture for three or four days. Then make a mixture of 25 percent old food and 75 percent new food. Feed this mixture for three or four days. Then you can start feeding 100 percent new food.

are six basic elements of nutrition: carbohydrates, fats, proteins, minerals, vitamins, and water.

## Carbohydrates

Carbohydrates fuel your puppy's body, giving him the get-up-and-go he needs to get through his day. However, if you overfeed your puppy or he doesn't get enough exercise he can become overweight.

In commercial dog foods, the major sources of carbohydrates are soluble carbohydrates consisting mainly of starches and sugars, introduced into your dog's diet primarily through cereal grains, such as rice, wheat, maize, barley, and oats. Insoluble carbohydrates, better known as fibre, come primarily from the cell walls of plants and grains, such as maize, soybean hulls, beet pulp, bran, and pectin. Fibre, while important in the diet, provides little in terms of energy or nutrition.

## Fats and Fatty Acids

Fats make food taste good, be it your yummy French fries or your dog's daily kibble. Fats provide a good source of food energy for your puppy, but they also contain approximately 2.25 times more metabolisable energy—the amount of energy in the food that is available to the dog—than do carbohydrates or proteins. Just like your own diet, you need to regulate your puppy's fat intake because if you feed too much fat and your puppy doesn't get enough exercise to burn all those calories, he can become overweight. At the other end of the spectrum, puppies who are fed ultra low-fat diets can develop health problems, such as dry, coarse hair and skin lesions.

Feed Me!

## Proteins and Amino Acids

Proteins are compounds of carbon, hydrogen, oxygen, and nitrogen arranged into a string of amino acids—much like the pearls on a necklace. Amino acids provide important building blocks that build strong muscles, ligaments, organs, bones, teeth, and coat. Your puppy cannot survive without protein because there are 10 specific amino acids that he cannot make on his own, and that means he must acquire them in his diet.

Not all proteins are created equal, however. Each protein is different in its ability to be broken down into amino acids, and dog food manufacturers use different types and qualities of protein that have varying degrees of digestibility. Some proteins have a higher biological value, meaning they are readily assimilated, or digested, so your puppy need not consume huge amounts. Foods that can't be digested adequately are wasted, passing through your puppy's system without providing optimum nutrition.

Chicken, beef, and lamb are the most common forms of protein used in dog foods. Other sources can include fish, fish meal, liver, milk, milk products, eggs, and soy. Some products, such as rice, wheat, maize, barley, and soy, also contain protein, but these plant proteins tend to be lower in quality than animal proteins because they must be combined with other proteins to yield complementary proteins that contain all the essential amino acids that puppies and adult dogs require.

## Vitamins

Vital to your puppy's health, vitamins do not provide energy, but, like

## Minerals

Minerals do not yield sources of energy, but they are important because they help regulate your puppy's complex system and are crucial components in energy metabolism. Essential nutrients are those that your puppy must obtain from food because his body cannot make them in sufficient quantity to meet physiological needs. Magnesium, potassium, and sodium, for example, are essential nutrients and important for nerve impulse transmission, muscle contraction and cell signalling, while calcium and phosphorous are important for strong bones and teeth.

Minerals are classified as *macro* or *micro* minerals depending on their concentration in the body. If dogs get too much or too little of a specific mineral in their diets, it can upset the delicate balance and cause serious health problems including tissue damage, convulsions, increased heart rate, anaemia, bone loss, and skeletal abnormalities. Never attempt to supplement minerals in your puppy's diet without professional advice from a veterinarian.

*Minerals help regulate your puppy's system.*

minerals, they are essential in the metabolic process. Certain vitamins are dependent on one another, and nearly every action in a dog's body requires the assistance of vitamins. Vitamin A, for example, is essential for vision, growth, foetal development, immune function, and transmembrane protein transfer. Vitamin $B_6$ is needed for glucose generation, red blood cell function, niacin synthesis, and gene activation.

While available through food sources, too much or too little of some vitamins can lead to serious health problems. Dogs fed diets lacking in Vitamin E, for example, may show signs of skeletal muscle breakdown, reproductive failure, and retinal degeneration. Excess amounts of vitamin D can cause anorexia, weakness, dehydration, muscle

atrophy, and excess mineralisation of long bones.

Vitamins are either water-soluble (B-complex and vitamin C) or fat-soluble (A, D, E, and K). Interestingly, dogs can make vitamin C from glucose, so they do not need to acquire it in their diet. Water-soluble vitamins must be replenished on a regular basis through diet. Fat-soluble vitamins are absorbed and stored in the body, which makes oversupplementation potentially dangerous. Always seek veterinary advice before supplementing with vitamins.

## Commercial Foods

Now that you are armed with the basics of canine nutrition, let's take a closer look at the different commercial meal options available and how you can choose the healthiest diet for your puppy. First and foremost, while seemingly endless options are available, and despite slick marketing tactics, no single food is "best." Some foods are top quality, some are better than others, and some are downright awful. The most expensive may not be the best, and rarely are the least expensive foods of good quality. You may need to try a few to see what works best for your dog.

Grocery shops, supermarkets, feed stores, and pet shops are the most convenient and popular locations for purchasing puppy and adult dog food. Veterinary surgeries also sell foods, and this is a good option, especially for dogs who require special diets, such as overweight dogs or dogs with allergies.

Commercial foods are undoubtedly the most convenient foods to buy, store, and use. The three most common types are tinned, dry, and semi-moist.

## Tinned Food

Chock full of chunky meats and delectable gravies, tinned foods are especially appealing to dogs. And they smell good, too! Okay, maybe not to you, but to your puppy, they smell wonderful. Available in an endless selection of flavours, combinations, and recipes, tinned foods are typically higher in fat and contain a higher meat protein level than do dry foods. They also have a high water content—up to 83 percent—with little grain, which makes the food more palatable than dry food.

Tinned food does have a few drawbacks, though. For starters, it is generally more expensive than dry food. The higher water content means that it has fewer nutrients than dry foods, so dogs must eat more to satisfy their energy and nutrient needs. Perhaps not a problem for, say, a Chihuahua or Yorkshire Terrier. However, it might prove too costly when it comes to feeding a Rottweiler, Great Dane, or Mastiff.

Tinned foods do not provide abrasion from chewing, which may allow faster plaque and tartar build-up on teeth. It can cause diarrhoea in some dogs. Once opened, tinned food is susceptible to spoilage, and leftovers must be refrigerated.

## Dry Food (Kibble)

High-quality premium dry foods tend to have high calorie density and good digestibility, meaning lower amounts per serving need to be consumed to satisfy a puppy's nutritional requirements. Convenient to buy, store, and feed, refrigeration is not required, and dry foods tend to have a long shelf life—around six months to one year. With moisture content between 6 and 10 percent, dry foods contain a high percentage of carbohydrates in the form of grain. Dental hygiene may be improved through chewing and grinding, although this is highly debatable among experts. They do, however, provide some exercise for your puppy's mouth and help to satisfy his need to chew.

*A high-quality puppy food should have all the nutrition your puppy needs.*

## Semi-Moist Food

High in moisture and sugar, semi-moist foods are lip-smacking good to most puppies and adult dogs. Too much sugar, however, may cause spikes in blood sugar levels and contribute to obesity—neither of which are good for your puppy. Generally marketed in sealed and resealable pouches, semi-moist foods come in all shapes and sizes. Ingredients can include fresh or frozen animal tissues, cereal, grains, fats, and simple sugar. Semi-moist foods may contain a number of chemicals and artificial colours.

## NonCommercial Diets

Premium commercial diets provide your puppy with a balanced, no-fuss diet. However, you may opt to feed a homemade diet or raw diet. If you love cooking for your family, then cooking for your puppy may not be too much extra work or trouble. Nevertheless, remember those important essential minerals and vitamins? They play an important part in your puppy's growth and development and, while not impossible, it can be hard to achieve the correct nutritional ratios on a daily basis when feeding a raw or homemade diet. Before jumping in, consider these other factors:

- Time-consuming and labour-intensive, homemade and raw diets can cut into your limited energy resources. Will you have the time or energy to cook Fido's dinner after a long day at the office? When the kids are sick? When the in-laws are visiting?

- Do you have adequate storage? Raw meats have no preservatives, so they must be stored in the refrigerator or freezer.

- Costly and often difficult to find, organic ingredients can tax your pocketbook. Are you willing to pay the extra money?

## The Expert Knows

### Water

Water is the single most important nutrient needed to sustain your four-legged friend's health. Water regulates your dog's temperature, supports metabolic reactions, allows blood to carry vital nutritional materials to cells, and removes waste products from your dog's system. The amount of water your puppy needs daily varies depending on environment, weather, activity, stress, and age. Rather than try to estimate how much water your puppy needs daily, provide him with an abundant supply of fresh, cool drinking water at all times. If you have less than desirable city water, consider a filtration system or purchase bottled water.

Feed Me!

- Canine nutrition is complicated. Some vitamins, such as vitamin D, are not only essential in small doses, but also toxic in excess amounts. Do you know enough to ensure your puppy is getting complete and balanced nutrients—including vitamins and minerals—on a daily basis?

That said, let's take a closer look at the pros and cons of both raw and homemade diets.

## Homemade Diet

Homemade diets are just that—meals made at home from scratch. Feeding natural or organic foods free of preservatives, additives, and who knows what else, are the primary reasons owners choose this route. Customising a dog's diet by providing a daily mixture of fresh meat, chicken, fish, vegetables, and occasionally commercial kibble, falls under the "pros" column of homemade diets. While not impossible, homemade diets are generally time-consuming, labour-

intensive, and complicated. Too much or too little, or the wrong combinations of nutrients or supplements, can be harmful to your puppy. Prudence dictates consulting with a canine nutritionist or veterinarian prior to feeding or changing any homemade diet.

## Raw Diet

BARF—Bones and Raw Food—is a popular acronym for this controversial diet of raw meat and bones, and opponents and proponents abound on both sides of the issue. In the simplest of terms, some people believe that drying, freezing, heating, or canning robs food of its nutritional components. Raw meat and bones, they believe, provide a more suitable diet for dogs, improving their dogs' skin, coat, and teeth, and allowing their pets to live longer and healthier lives and have better immune systems.

Opponents caution against bacterial infections, parasites, and food-borne illnesses for both dogs and humans when handling and eating raw food, such as raw meat, poultry, eggs, and unprocessed milk. Also, dogs who eat bones are susceptible to choking or stomach damage.

Some dog food manufacturers now sell raw diets in pet and specialty shops. Usually found in the freezer section, these diets are individually packaged to make feeding simple.

As with the homemade diet, checking with your vet is always a good idea before embarking on a new diet for your puppy.

*Commercial foods are a convenient feeding option.*

## Feeding Requirements

Nutritional and calorie requirements, as well as eating habits, differ between puppies and adult dogs. As previously mentioned, puppies grow rapidly. Their systems are busy building strong muscles, bones, and vital organs, and establishing a resistance to disease—all of which requires energy. For the first six to twelve months of your puppy's life, he needs a specially formulated growth food designed exclusively for these greater energy and nutritional needs.

Puppies have smaller stomachs, too, so they must be fed smaller amounts of food three or four times a day until they are about six months of age. From six months to one year of age and thereafter, you should feed your puppy two times a day—once in the morning and again in the evening. Again, these feeding schedules are guidelines, and they will differ slightly from dog to dog.

## How Much?

Getting the feeding schedule down pat is only half the battle. Next you'll need to feed the correct amount of food, and that's a bit tricky because puppy growth rates and appetites are primarily dictated by genetics and vary from puppy to puppy—even among littermates.

The feeding guidelines on puppy foods will help you establish a starting point. However, dog food manufactures tend to be overly generous with their proportions. Feed enough food to meet your puppy's individual nutritional

# FAMILY-FRIENDLY TIP

## Toxic Foods

Kids, snacks, and dogs seem to go hand-in-hand. However, dogs have a metabolism that is different from humans, and some foods (and nonfood items) can cause serious health problems, ranging from upset stomach to death. Teach your child to never feed unapproved doggie snacks including these yummy human foods:

- Bones from fish, poultry, or other meat sources.
- Cat food—while not fatal—is high in protein and fat and particularly appetising to puppies.
- Chocolate
- Grapes and raisins
- Macadamia nuts
- Mushrooms
- Onions and garlic
- Raw eggs, milk, and other dairy products

This is a small sampling of foods that are toxic to dogs. Seek veterinary attention immediately if you suspect your puppy has ingested a toxic substance.

33

Feed Me!

requirements, but don't feed so much that he gets fat. It's a balancing act, and you need to ration his food according to his needs, not his wants, because some puppies are greedier than others and will almost always want more food.

Equally important, different breeds reach maturity at different ages. Generally speaking, smaller breeds tend to reach adulthood sooner than large breeds. Adult foods, often called maintenance diets, are specially designed foods that satisfy the energy and nutritional needs of adult dogs who have reached maturity. Switching from a puppy to adult food will depend on your dog's individual nutritional requirements. Your veterinarian is a good source for determining the proper amount and type of food to feed.

## Scheduled Versus Free Feeding

Scheduled feeding, which is highly recommended, and free-feeding, which is more convenient for you but not nearly as beneficial to your puppy, are your two choices when it comes to feeding your puppy. Both have their pros and cons. Let's take a closer look.

## Scheduled Feeding

Establishing a regular routine of eating and toileting is the essence of scheduled feeding. Ideally, you should feed your puppy at regular times, then pick up whatever food is left after 10 minutes. Refrigerate any perishable food or toss leftovers to prevent spoilage. This regimen establishes a regular routine of eating

and toileting, which helps speed up the housetraining process because what goes in on a regular basis comes out on a regular basis. Equally important, scheduled feeding helps to avoid obesity in your puppy. Juvenile obesity increases the number of fat cells in a puppy and predisposes him to obesity for the rest of his life.

## Free-Feeding

Putting your puppy's food out, leaving it all day, and allowing your puppy to eat at his leisure, is not recommended. While more convenient for you, it does not establish a set schedule for feeding and toileting. Most puppies—and adult dogs—will eat and eat and eat, as long as food is available. After a good vomit, they gleefully start all over again. Food-bowl guarding is one of the potential—not to mention dangerous—

*Keep an eye on how much your puppy is eating—just a few extra treats can lead to a weight problem.*

side effects of free-feeding, as is dog-to-dog squabbling, which even the best of friends are not immune to. In a multiple-dog household, it is best to confine all the dogs separately in crates or kennels while they eat. Otherwise, you will not know for certain if your puppy is eating or his canine brothers and sisters are eating for him.

## Obesity

Being a responsible pet owner includes not allowing your puppy to become overweight. Juvenile obesity increases the number of fat cells in a puppy and predisposes him to obesity for the rest of his life. However, keeping your dog lean and within an acceptable weight range for his size can increase his lifespan by nearly two years!

Unfortunately, experts indicate that as more and more owners become overweight, so too do their dogs. Diabetes, increased blood pressure, congestive heart failure, and digestive disorders are a few of the weight-related diseases that can affect dogs, as well as humans. Extra fat restricts the expansion of a dog's lungs, making breathing difficult. Regulating their body temperature is more difficult for overweight dogs, thereby making them more susceptible to heatstroke than their lean counterparts.

Overweight dogs have less stamina and endurance because their heart, muscles, and respiratory system are working overtime. Your veterinarian can help you determine the ideal weight for your dog and develop a long-term plan to condition his

### Is My Puppy Overweight?

Keep your dog's weight on track by using these simple weekly guidelines for assessing his weight:
- Run your fingers up and down his rib cage. You should be able to feel the bumps of his rib cage without pressing in.
- Run your hand over his croup (his rump). You should be able to feel the bumps of his two pelvic bones with little effort and without pressing down.
- If your have trouble feeling his ribs or pelvic bones, or if your feel fat deposits on his back, hip region, spine, chest, shoulders, neck, and legs, or his belly looks distended, seek veterinary care to help develop an exercise and nutritional programme for slimming down.

Feed Me!

body and provide him with a longer, healthier life.

# Chapter 4

# Groom Me!

Grooming should be a regular part of your puppy's routine. If started earlier on, when your puppy is still young and more receptive to new experiences, grooming becomes an enjoyable part of his routine—just like eating, sleeping, and playing.

Regular grooming keeps his skin and coat in tip-top condition, and allows you to check his entire body for lumps, bumps, cuts, rashes, dry skin, fleas, ticks, stickers, and the like. You can check his feet for cuts, torn pads, or broken nails, and examine his mouth for signs of trouble including tartar, broken teeth, or discoloured gums.

A key to success is to keep the sessions short and positive, and progress at a rate that is suitable for the age and mental maturity of your puppy. If your puppy came from a reputable breeder, chances are good that he is used to being handled and gently stroked. He's probably had at least one bath and may already be accustomed to and tolerate being brushed and examined. Exposing your puppy to positive and delightful grooming experiences will help your puppy grow into an adult dog who takes pleasure in this necessary chore.

Most puppies love to be groomed, making this task a great way to spend quality time with your puppy while simultaneously building a strong and mutually trusting human–canine relationship.

## Coat Care

Your puppy's coat type will dictate how much care and daily grooming is required.

### Curly Coats

Curly-coated breeds, like Poodles and Bichons Frises, require a lot of upkeep for their curly locks. Scissors and clippers are must-have tools for these breeds. Many people who own these breeds use a professional groomer to keep their puppy in tip-top shape.

### Double Coats

Many breeds such as Shetland Sheepdogs, Welsh Terriers, and Lhasa Apsos have two coats, which can usually stand up to a bit more abuse around the house and on the road than can their silky-soft-coated counterparts. However, they still require regular grooming. Referred to as double-coated or two-ply coated, the undercoat is usually short, soft, and dense—acting as a protective layer against water and the elements. The top coat, or outer coat, is generally longer, and varies in texture depending on the breed. If not regularly groomed out, the undercoat gets thick and matted and can be extremely uncomfortable for the dog.

### Hairless

A few hairless breeds exist, including the rare Peruvian Inca Orchid Dog, the American Hairless Terrier, and the Chinese Crested (hairless variety). While hairless breeds do not require

*Getting your pup used to being touched will help with the grooming process.*

brushing, skin care and protection are major concerns.

## Long- or Drop-Coats

Long- or drop-coated breeds, such as the Maltese or Yorkshire Terrier, require special attention, since their hair drapes down their body nearly or all the way to the ground. Keeping up appearances with this type of breed requires extra commitment. The hair is highly susceptible to damage and breakage caused by harsh shampoos, excessive blow-drying, and exposure to environmental elements. Every aspect—from brushing and bathing to housing—requires special attention to maintain these sensitive yet exquisite coats.

**The Expert Knows**

### Accepting Grooming

Puppies have limited attentions spans, so do not expect your puppy to remain still for extended periods. In the beginning, you want progress—not perfection. Your goal is for him to stand or lie still for a few seconds while you praise him. Harsh handling during these learning stages will come back to haunt you when your puppy begins to resent this necessary chore. Progress to the point where your puppy will accept having his body stroked with your hand, then gently, slowly, and calmly brush him all over. In the beginning, your puppy may be frightened, nervous, or unsure. Patience, gentle handling, and plenty of hugs and kisses will help to build his confidence and teach him to accept and enjoy the grooming process.

## Rough Coats

Some breeds, are considered "rough coated," which is a bit misleading because they are not always rough or harsh to the touch. The Border Collies' rough coat, for example, is medium to long with a flat to slightly wavy texture. The rough-coat Collie, on the other hand, has a coat that is straight and harsh to the touch. Either way, rough-coats also require regular care and maintenance, preferably on a daily basis.

## Single Coats

Single-coated breeds, such as the Italian Greyhound, Portuguese Water Dog, and Bichon Frise have no undercoat. While these dogs may be easier to brush than double coats, they still require regular grooming to keep their coats in tip-top condition.

## Smooth Coats

Smooth-coated dogs, depending on the breed, can be either single- or double-coated. The smooth-coated Border Collie, smooth variety Collie, and smooth-coated Chihuahua, for example, have undercoats, whereas the smooth-coated Vizla has no undercoat. Smooth-coated breeds are often referred to as "wash and wear" breeds, but they too require regular bathing and grooming to remove dead hair and debris.

## Wire Coats

Many terriers have wiry or wire-haired coats, which, as the name implies, are harsh, crinkly, and wiry coats. With the exception of a few die-hard terrier enthusiasts who continue to hand "pluck" a Terriers' coat—meaning they pluck or pull old or excess hair out by hand—most Terriers kept as pets are stripped by a groomer using a stripping knife.

## Combination Coats

Mixed-breed dogs often have a combination-type coat, as do some of the mixed-breed "designer" dogs. The Goldendoodle, for example, which can be a groomer's nightmare, has a soft undercoat similar to that of the Golden Retriever and a soft Poodle topcoat, which is not unlike trying to comb through cotton. These coats require regular care and maintenance to prevent painful mats.

## Brushing

Correct brushing is the most critical grooming skill needed.

## Equipment

Countless types of brushes—from slickers to boar hair to wire pin—are available, and the equipment you choose depends largely on your dog's breed.

- Slicker: works well for removing dead undercoat and debris from double-coated breeds; should

never be used on the long hair of a drop-coated breed because it can cause breakage

- Soft metal pin brush: base should be rubber-cushioned; pins should give and not break the hair; good for a variety of coats because they can work through the top and undercoats easily
- Metal comb: can be used to help break up mats and help remove stubborn undercoats
- Curry comb, grooming mitt, and canine chamois: good for going over smooth-coated breeds

## How To Brush Your Puppy

Regardless of your dog's coat type, you should start brushing at the dog's head—brushing the top of the head and around the ears, down the neck, chest, and front legs. Then brush in one long stroke from the head toward the tail; brush down the sides, and finish with the rear legs. Many groomers discourage backward brushing—brushing against the direction of hair growth—because it can damage the coat, and some dogs find the process uncomfortable and annoying. Finish off smooth-coated breeds by rubbing them down with a chamois or soft towel and spraying or rubbing on a coat oil, which will add shine.

When brushing medium- to long-haired breeds, keep damage to a minimum by brushing gently; don't tug or pull because this can hurt. Part the hair with one hand and work from the skin out, brushing only in the direction of the hair growth, and continue right to the ends. Avoid "flicking" the ends of the hair, which can lead to breakage. Always mist or spray the hair first with a diluted mixture of cream rinse and water or a coat conditioner to help control static and prevent breakage.

Be sure to brush down to the skin, brushing both the top coat and undercoat. Brushing only the top coat can result in painful mats and tangles that are difficult, if not impossible, to comb out. When a matted coat gets wet, the moisture is trapped near the skin, causing hot spots—circular lesions that are inflamed, raw, moist, and very painful.

It goes without saying that the vast number of coat types and lengths requires varying degrees of grooming

41

*Examples of a double-coat (Sheltie, left); long-coat (Yorkie, centre); single-coat (Italian Greyhound, right).*

techniques and daily, weekly, and monthly care—all of which goes beyond the scope of this book. When in doubt, always seek advice from your puppy's breeder or from a professional groomer.

## Bathing

Like kids, some dogs have a knack for getting dirtier than others. How often your puppy requires bathing depends on where you live, how much time he spends outside, and how dirty he gets.

In hot climates, you may be able to bathe your dog outdoors with a garden hose, provided the water is not too cold. Otherwise, a rubber mat on the bottom of a bath or shower stall will provide secure footing and prevent him from slipping. Don't forget about slippery floors, either. A rubber mat or plenty of dry towels on the bathroom floor will prevent your puppy from slipping and injuring himself. Have plenty of towels on hand for cleaning up and drying off.

## How to Bathe Your Puppy

Saturate your puppy's coat, undercoat (if he has one), and skin with lukewarm water. Apply a dab or two of shampoo and scrub away. Work the shampoo into the coat with your fingers or a rubber massage tool designed specifically for dogs. Scrub from head to toe, being careful to avoid the eye area. Don't overlook his belly, the inside of his hind legs, under his arms, and behind his ears. To clean around a puppy's eyes, wipe the eye area with a damp cloth. Tearless shampoos are available for washing around the head and eye area but, even though it is tearless, avoid getting any in your dog's eyes.

Rinse his entire body thoroughly with lukewarm water until the water runs clear. Rinsing is the most important part because some coats can hold a lot of suds, and residual shampoo can irritate the skin, as well as leave a dull film on the coat. If necessary, shampoo and rinse again to be sure your puppy is squeaky clean. If you are using a coat conditioner or skin moisturiser, follow directions carefully.

## Drying

If possible, let your puppy shake off any extra water, then towel dry him thoroughly. Take care to protect him from any drafts

*A pin brush is useful for brushing many types of coats.*

## Secrets of Proper Shampooing

Countless brands of shampoos and conditioners are available, and they can either enhance and complement individual coats or detract and depreciate them by stripping them of natural oils, weighing them down, or gumming them up. The breed of dog you have chosen will dictate the type of shampoo and conditioner you choose. Yorkies, for example, tend to have a lot of natural oils in their coat, so their silky coat requires a minimal amount of conditioner, otherwise you'll end up with a dog that is very greasy looking. A Lhasa Apso, on the other hand, has a heavy, textured undercoat and a coarse outer coat that requires a conditioner for some shine and to eliminate static, yet not so much as to soften the coat.

Unless your puppy has a specific skin condition, such as dry, flaky, itchy skin, choose a good quality shampoo and conditioner designed specifically for dogs—something nontoxic and soap-based, rather than detergent-based, so as not to strip the hair of its natural oils. Many shampoos and conditioning products are available, from all-purpose to medicating to herbal to colour-enhancing, so do not be shy about asking for help when choosing shampoos and conditioners.

or getting chilled. If you live where temperatures are warm, and your puppy is likely to air dry quickly, blow-drying may not be necessary. If you choose to complete the process by blow-drying, hold the dryer at least 6 inches (15 cm) away from the coat, keep the dryer in motion, and use a low or cool setting to avoid damaging the coat or burning your puppy's skin.

## Dental Care

Taking good care of your puppy's teeth is paramount. If not well cared for, your dog can develop periodontal disease, a progressive disease than can lead to decayed teeth, gum infection, and liver, kidney, and heart disease.

## Getting Started

Ideally, as with other aspects of grooming, you should begin exposing your puppy to the practice of oral hygiene at an early age, but it is never to late to begin—just start slowly and progress at a pace suitable for your puppy.

Puppies often struggle with having their mouths examined because they are unfamiliar with the routine, and their mouth and gums can be super sensitive, especially when they are teething—when the adult teeth begin pushing through the gums, which generally occurs between four and six months of age, but can vary from dog to dog.

You will need a pet toothbrush or a finger toothbrush, and toothpaste designed specifically for dogs. Most canine toothpastes are formulated with poultry- or malt-flavoured enhancers for easier acceptance. A word of caution: Never use human toothpaste because it can upset your puppy's stomach.

Start by using your finger to massage your puppy's gums. Put a small dab of doggie toothpaste on your index finger, and let your puppy lick it. Praise him for being brave! Apply another dab on your finger, gently lift up his outer lips, and massage his gums.

Ideally, it is best to massage in a circular motion but, in the beginning, you may need to be satisfied with simply getting your finger in your puppy's mouth—without getting bitten by those razor-sharp baby teeth. Try to massage top and bottom, and the front gums, too. Keep a positive attitude, praising and reassuring your puppy throughout the process. Try to avoid wrestling with your puppy or restraining him too tightly. This will only hamper the process and make him resistant to this chore.

## The Next Step

Depending on your puppy, it may take a few days or a few weeks for him to accept you fiddling about in his mouth. Once your puppy is comfortable with the process, try using the toothbrush or finger toothbrush. Let your puppy lick some toothpaste off the toothbrush and, again, praise him for being brave.

You are now ready to begin brushing. As before, lift the outer lips—being careful not to pinch his lips—and expose the teeth. Most owners find it easiest to start with the canine teeth—the large ones in the front of the mouth. They are the easiest to reach and, with any luck, you should be able to brush them with little interference or objection from your puppy. Once your puppy is accustomed to your brushing a few teeth, progress to a few more, then a few more until

*How often you bathe your puppy depends on how much time he spends outside.*

you have brushed all 28 puppy teeth (42 teeth if your puppy is older and has his permanent teeth). Remember to always progress at a pace that is suitable for your puppy.

In addition to regular at-home brushings, provide your puppy with plenty of chew or dental toys that help to remove plaque. Toys should not replace brushing, but they will help to remove some of the plaque, exercise your puppy's jaw, and satisfy his need to chew.

Equally important, you will want to have your puppy's teeth professionally cleaned by your veterinarian at least once a year.

## Ear Care

To clean your puppy's ears, place a few drops of ear cleaner—a product specifically designed for dogs—in the puppy's ear canal and gently massage the base of the ear for about 20 seconds. This helps to soften and loosen debris. When you're done, let your puppy have a good head shake to eject the cleaning solution and debris from the ear canal. Next, apply some ear-cleaning solution onto a clean cotton or gauze pad. Gently wipe the inside ear leather (ear flap), and the part of the ear canal that you can see.

Remember the old adage, "Never stick anything smaller than your elbow in your ear?" The same concept applies to your puppy. Never stick cotton applicator swabs or pointed objects into the ear canal because this tends to pack the debris rather than remove it. Most important, you risk injuring your puppy's

## FAMILY-FRIENDLY TIP

### Children and Grooming

Children—especially the younger ones who are always willing to lend a helping hand—make great grooming assistants. Supervision is always necessary, and brushing is a great place to start if you have a smooth-coat or medium-coat breed because the coat is shorter and easy to brush. Children should learn to brush in one direction, brushing the entire dog from head to tail. Let children smell the puppy's ears to be sure they smell clean and fresh— kind of like beeswax. Let her sound the alarm if your puppy has dirty eyes or long nails.

For smaller kids, stand them in the bath and let them scrub away with plenty of shampoo. Teach them not to be too rough or boisterous, so as not to scare the puppy. Once the puppy is thoroughly rinsed, they can help apply the conditioner, rinse him again, then help dry him.

Letting your child assist with grooming responsibility teaches her about responsibility and compassion and helps her to build a mutually respectful and loving relationship with her puppy.

45

Groom Me!

eardrum should you probe too deeply.

## Preventing Ear Problems

The key to preventing ear problems is to keep ears clean, and to know the difference between a clean-smelling ear and a problem ear. A healthy ear should have a clean, healthy doggy smell—resembling the smell of beeswax, somewhat. Honey-coloured wax in the ear is normal, but a crusty, dark substance may indicate problems, such as ear mites. An infected ear has a foul odour. Ear infections are serious, and should never be ignored or taken lightly. If your puppy's ears have a discharge, smell bad, the canals look abnormal, red, or inflamed; or your dog is showing signs of discomfort, such as depression or irritability, scratching or rubbing his ears or head, shaking his head or tilting it to one side—these are signs of a problem. Seek veterinary attention right away. An ear infection left untreated can cause permanent damage to your puppy's hearing.

## Eye Care

Your puppy's eyes should be clear and bright. Clean his eyes by saturating a gauze pad or soft wash cloth with warm water; starting at the inside of the eye, gently wipe out toward the outside corner of the eye. If you notice excessive tearing, redness, swelling, discolouration, or discharge, these may be signs of an infection. If you suspect something is wrong, do not hesitate to call your veterinarian.

## Nail Care

Trimming your puppy's nails is another important and necessary part of dog ownership. Nails that are too long interfere with a puppy's gait—making walking awkward and painful. Long nails can be broken, torn off, or snagged and can scratch furniture, hardwood floors, and skin. Torn or broken nails can cause a puppy a great deal of pain and discomfort, and they may become infected, which can require veterinary attention.

Like other aspects of grooming, it is always best to start while your puppy is young and receptive to new experiences. With any luck, the breeder will have started nipping small pieces of nail as part of the socialisation process, as well as to build the puppy's confidence and teach him to accept having his feet handled. In the beginning, depending on your puppy's level of cooperation, you may want to simply touch the nail clipper to the puppy's nails and then offer plenty of praise. Then progress to clipping tiny bits of nail during each session. It isn't necessary to clip all his nails in one sitting.

## How to Cut Your Puppy's Nails

Dogs have a blood vessel—known as the "quick"—that travels approximately three-quarters of the way through the nail. Clipping a dog's nails too short can cut the quick and cause bleeding. Puppies—depending on the breed—may have white or black nails or a combination. Black nails can make it difficult to differentiate between the quick and the hook—the dead section of nail that extends beyond the quick.

Examine the underside of the nail before clipping. The section closest to the paw is solid, while the tip—or hook—of the nail looks hollow, like a shell. You may be able to see or feel the slightest groove on the underside hook portion of the nail. Trim only the portion between the solid nail and the thinner hollow part—just tipping it where it curves slightly downward.

One of the easiest ways to start trimming a young puppy's nails is to hold him in your lap. While he's nibbling on a chunk of yummy food (i.e., cheese, turkey, steak), have someone trim his nails. Praise with "Good boy!" each time a nail is clipped, which creates a positive, nontraumatic experience. In time, gradually progress to holding him yourself or having him sit, stand, or lie down on the grooming table. It is really a matter of preference, what is easiest for you, and what your puppy will and will not tolerate. If you find you simply cannot trim his nails, take him to a veterinarian or groomer for regular nail clippings, which, depending on how fast his nails grow, can mean once a week, once a month, or somewhere in between.

## Dewclaws

Dewclaws are the fifth digit on the inside of the front legs, usually an inch or so above the feet. Be sure not to overlook them during the trimming process. If left unattended, they can curl around and grow into the soft tissue. Some breeders have the dewclaws removed when the puppy is very young, so your puppy may or may not have them.

*When trimming your puppy's nails, avoid cutting the quick.*

# Chapter 5

# Keep Me
# Healthy!

Your puppy is counting on you to take care of him—especially when he is sick. A number of serious illnesses can hamper your puppy's well being, and some breeds are prone or predisposed to certain illnesses or diseases. Being able to recognise when your puppy is feeling a bit under the weather or facing a serious medical emergency is an important component of canine ownership.

Just as you pay close attention to any symptoms that might indicate your child has a cold or something more serious, such as the measles or chicken pox, you need to know how to recognise when something is amok with your puppy. Understanding what is normal will help you to recognise when something is amiss, and it will ensure that your adorable puppy grows into a healthy, happy adult dog.

### Choosing a Veterinarian

Now that you have a great puppy, you need a great veterinarian! Finding one takes a bit of time, but do yourself and your puppy a favour by locating a suitable veterinarian with whom you feel comfortable asking questions, sharing concerns, and building a mutually trusting and respectful relationship before you need one. Plan ahead—scanning the telephone book when your puppy is sick or injured is never a good idea.

### Where to Look

Breeders are often a good starting point. Most reputable breeders know several local veterinarians and specialists. If you acquired your puppy from a breeder, chances are good that the veterinarians recommended by the breeder are familiar with your breed.

Local telephone directories are a good starting point, too, as are animal-owning friends, relatives, neighbours, and co-workers. Ask around at local breed clubs, shows, or training facilities. Experienced dog people frequent these places, and they always have on hand the names and numbers of first-rate veterinarians. Finally, ask your current veterinarian to refer you to some veterinarians if you are moving to a new town.

### Check Out the Facilities

Proximity to your home, surgery hours, cleanliness of the facility, services offered, and whether you prefer a male or female veterinarian are personal preferences that generally dictate or heavily influence your decision when it comes to choosing a veterinary clinic that best suits you and your puppy. Some clinics offer boarding kennels, grooming services, and retail shopping. Others offer weekend and after-hour emergency care.

Once you have narrowed down your selection, tour the clinic. Ask questions about their day-to-day protocol, billing

*Your kids can learn a lot by visiting the vet with your puppy.*

policies, surgery hours, and after-hours emergency care policy. Do they make house calls? In multi-doctor clinics, can you request a specific veterinarian? Are they knowledgeable, courteous, friendly, and receptive to your concerns?

Tour the entire facility, including exam rooms, x-ray room, the operating and recovery rooms, and the boarding areas—all of which should be as neat and tidy as any military base. Are there unpleasant odours? Is the clinic organised? Noisy? Chaotic? Does the waiting area provide adequate room for separating large and small dogs, unruly dogs from nervous dogs, and rambunctious dogs from shy dogs? What about a fenced grassy area where your puppy can relieve himself?

The relationship between you and your veterinarian is as important as the relationship between you and your own doctor. So take your time and choose one with whom you will be comfortable for the next 10 to 15 years.

## Puppy's First Visit

Your puppy's first visit should be fun and enjoyable, so be sure to leave any anxiety and trepidation at home. But do bring a pocket full of treats to reward your puppy for being brave! Most veterinarians have excellent bedside manners, and they want your puppy's first—and subsequent—visit to be a positive experience.

Ideally, plan on scheduling your puppy's first visit within 48 to72 hours of acquiring him, to make sure he has no health problems. To the untrained

## FAMILY-FRIENDLY TIP

### Visiting the Vet with Your Child

Your puppy is going to require several visits to the veterinarian's— especially for his puppy shots, annual wellness visits, and routine teeth cleanings. Bringing your child along will help her to learn about responsibility and the importance of taking good care of the family pet. Making the visit a positive experience for you, your child, and your puppy means planning ahead. For example, read basic canine healthcare books with her. Explain why your puppy will be going to the vet's surgery, and have her jot down a few questions to ask the veterinarian, such as how much her dog should weigh, how tall he should be, how often his nails need trimming, or how old the dog really is in human years.  Also, jot down some information that your child can give to the veterinarian, such as how often you feed the dog, how much and what type of food, how often he goes to the bathroom, and so forth. Most clinics are accepting of well-behaved children, and veterinarians are usually willing to answer questions about their equipment, procedures, and so forth.

51

Keep Me Healthy!

eye, a seemingly normal-looking puppy can have medical problems. Looking for anything out of the ordinary, the veterinarian will check your puppy's overall condition, including inspecting his skin, coat, eyes, ears, feet, lymph nodes, glands, teeth, and gums. She will take his temperature and pulse, listen to his heart and lungs, and feel his abdomen, muscles, and joints. She also should ask about your puppy's eating and toilet habits.

Jot down any relevant information beforehand so that you have it at your fingertips, such as the type of food your puppy eats, how much and how often he eats, how often he relieves himself, the colour, shape, and size of his stools, and so forth. It's a good idea to bring a fresh stool sample with you so that your veterinarian can check it for parasites. Put the stool sample in

a plastic bag or disposable container, and place the container inside a brown paper bag labelled with your name and your puppy's name.

Make a list of any questions you want to ask, such as how much and what type of food your puppy should be eating, how often he should eat, health concerns particular to your breed, vaccinations, neutering, the name of a good puppy trainer, and so forth. Be proactive in your puppy's health and well-being by asking questions. Take advantage of this time to establish a good relationship with your vet and her staff.

## Vaccinations

Like people, puppies need vaccinations, too. No doubt you were vaccinated against measles, mumps, and a host of other diseases when you were a young child, to help keep you healthy. Your puppy needs vaccinations to keep him healthy, too, because a number of highly contagious and deadly canine diseases can make him very sick.

Vaccines trigger immune responses in your puppy's body and prepare him to fight future infections from disease-causing agents. They protect not only your puppy but other puppies, too, by helping to control the spread of infectious diseases.

Vaccinations generally start being administered at eight weeks of age and continue every three weeks until the puppy is sixteen weeks of age. However, your veterinarian will tailor a programme of vaccinations to help your puppy grow into a happy, healthy

*Vaccinations have saved the lives of millions of dogs.*

adult dog. Your puppy's lifestyle, where you live, and how much travelling you plan to do will factor into your puppy's vaccination plan. For years, annual vaccinations or booster shots were considered normal. However, science and technology have helped experts learn more about diseases and your puppy's immunity. Increasing evidence suggests immunity from today's vaccines may last beyond one year.

The breeder from whom you acquired your puppy may have administered your puppy's first puppy shots. If so, you should have received a copy of the date and type of vaccine. Take this information with you on your puppy's first vet visit. Veterinarians differ in their vaccination protocol, but most inoculate against the following seven most common diseases.

- **Coronavirus:** Spread through the stool of infected dogs, coronavirus is highly contagious. Rarely fatal to adult dogs but frequently fatal to puppies, symptoms include vomiting, loss of appetite, and diarrhoea, which may lead to dehydration, further endangering puppies. Puppies less than twelve weeks of age are at the greatest risk.

- **Distemper:** A primary cause of illness and death in unvaccinated puppies, distemper is a highly contagious viral disease similar to the virus that causes measles in humans. Spread through the air as well as through contact with an

## An Optional Shot: Lyme Disease

Depending on where you live, your veterinarian may choose to vaccinate against Lyme disease—a bacterial infection caused by a slender spiral microorganism identified as *Borrelia burgdorferi*. Transmitted to humans and dogs through the bite of an infected deer tick, illness may not show up for months after initial exposure to an infected tick, and the severity of the disease may vary depending on the dog's age and immune status.

53

Keep Me Healthy!

infected animal's stool or urine, distemper can spread rapidly through kennels or multiple-dog households. Symptoms include nasal and eye discharge, coughing, diarrhoea, vomiting, and seizures. Distemper is an incurable and deadly disease that can affect dogs of all age; however, puppies and senior dogs are most vulnerable.

- **Hepatitis:** Spread primarily through direct contact with an infected dog's saliva, nasal discharge, and urine, infectious canine hepatitis is caused by an adenovirus. Unvaccinated dogs of all ages are at risk. The mortality rate is high, but vaccination prevents the disease.

- **Leptospirosis:** A highly contagious bacterial disease, leptospirosis is spread primarily through the urine of infected animals. Vaccinations usually prevent the disease, although leptospirosis does appear in different strains, and vaccination against one strain does not protect against all strains.

- **Kennel Cough:** Also known as canine infectious tracheobronchitis or *Bordetellosis,* kennel cough is a highly contagious airborne disease and can spread rapidly among dogs who live together. Dogs at shows, boarding kennels, grooming shops, veterinary clinics, and public or private parks are at an increased risk to exposure.

- **Parvovirus:** A life-threatening virus, parvo is spread through the stools of infected dogs. The majority of puppies infected are under six months of age, with the most severe cases seen in puppies younger than twelve weeks of age. Mortality rates are high, but vaccination helps prevent the disease.

- **Rabies:** This highly infectious viral disease affects all warm-blooded animals—humans included. Mortality is high, and the disease is almost always fatal once symptoms appear. Transmission is generally

# Spaying and Neutering: Why It's a Good Idea

Before long, your cute and cuddly puppy will grow into an adorable adult dog who is capable of reproducing. Regardless of his (or her) eye-catching good looks and intelligence, not allowing your dog to reproduce is one of the most important and responsible roles of canine ownership. A lot of owners have an aversion to spaying or neutering their puppy. Rest assured, your puppy will not care one iota that he is neutered. He won't get fat—unless you let him. He won't hate you. He won't hold a grudge. He won't be less of a companion and, contrary to public opinion, he won't even know his "parts" are missing. Females will not make better pets simply because they are allowed to whelp "just one litter."

Spaying or neutering helps your puppy to live a longer and healthier life. Spaying females helps reduce mammary gland tumours, ovarian and uterine infections, and cancer, and it decreases the incidence of female aggression. Castrating males helps reduce prostate disease, testicular cancer, leg lifting, roaming, aggression, and marking (peeing on anything and everything in sight!).

Spaying and neutering reduces pet overpopulation and keeps your dog healthy by reducing a number of medical and behavioural problems. It's as simple as that.

through the bite of a rabid animal. No cure is available. Vaccination is the best way to prevent infection, and will be necessary if you are travelling with your puppy overseas.

*Good breeding is one of the best ways to ensure a healthy pup.*

## Parasites

Few topics are as grotesque as parasites! Being an informed pet owner means educating yourself about these pesky creatures because, if you own a puppy, chances are high that sometime within his lifetime he will suffer from an external parasite (like fleas) or an internal parasite (like worms). Puppies also get mites and mange, but that isn't necessarily a reflection of your stellar housekeeping skills. If left unchecked, parasites can wreak havoc with your puppy, causing debilitating and life-threatening problems.

### External Parasites

Fleas and ticks are a real problem for puppies and adult dogs because they can get out of control very quickly. One flea can bite your dog up to 400 times a day! Keeping one step ahead of these pesky creatures is the best way to ensure your puppy stays happy, healthy, and comfortable.

### *Fleas*

About 1/8-inch (0.3-cm) long and slightly smaller than a sesame seed, these tiny pests can send your puppy into a vicious cycle of scratching, biting, and digging at his skin. And

where one flea exists, chances are high that plenty more are lurking on your precious puppy—as well as in your carpet, furniture, and bedding.

The *Ctenocephalides felis*, also known as the domestic cat flea, is the most common flea responsible for infesting dogs, spreading tapeworms, and causing serious allergic dermatitis. Fleas also can, in serious infestations, cause anaemia, especially in puppies.

The good news is that the advent of once-a-month topical treatments makes eradicating fleas a lot easier than it was ten or fifteen years ago. Applied to the dog's skin between the shoulder blades, these liquid treatments are absorbed into your dog's system, and the flea is killed when it bites the dog.

Additionally, a number of shampoos, sprays, dips, and powders are available. While they have been around for years, many commercial and natural products may be toxic. They may irritate your puppy's skin or cause health problems.

Flea-control products are most effective when used in conjunction with a rigorous flea-control regimen. A flea collar alone will not provide your puppy with a flea-free environment.

### Ticks

Utterly dreadful, ticks burrow their head into your puppy's skin and engorge themselves with blood, expanding to many times their size. They can secret a paralysis-causing toxin and can spread serious diseases, including Lyme disease. Ticks can also be infected with and transmit more than one disease. In severe infestations, anaemia and even death may occur.

Approximately 850 species of ticks exist, and most are picked up while walking or playing in wooded or grassy areas, overgrown fields, and near low, overhanging branches or shrubs. Ticks commonly embed themselves between the toes, in the ears, and around the neck but can be found elsewhere on your puppy's body.

Controlling ticks is very similar to controlling fleas. Treat your house, garden, dog blankets and beds, and your dog with products designed specifically for ticks. A number of over-the-counter products are available, but again, these products may be toxic. Read all labels and follow directions carefully.

If you find a tick on your puppy, remove it immediately. This isn't terribly difficult—once you get past any queasiness about doing so. Use tweezers or a specially designed tick-removing tool to grab the tick as close as possible to where it enters your puppy's skin. Pull slowly, firmly, and steadily in an outward direction. Clean the bite wound with a disinfectant and apply an antibiotic ointment. Dispose of the tick by immersing it in rubbing alcohol. If you simply cannot bring yourself to remove the tick, take your puppy to the veterinarian. Ticks must be removed, and the sooner the better.

## Internal Parasites

Endoparasites live inside your puppy's body. Endo means *in*, hence their catchy name. Heartworms, hookworms, roundworms, tapeworms, and whipworms, are the most common, and all are capable of causing problems with your puppy's health and well-being. Deworming medications are available at pet shops and retail outlets. However, dewormers differ drastically

*Check your puppy for fleas and ticks after he's been outside.*

in their safety and effectiveness in expelling worms from a dog's body. So always have your veterinarian diagnose the specific type of internal parasite and prescribe the proper deworming medication.

- **Heartworms:** Transmitted by mosquitoes, heartworms are dangerous and deadly internal parasites because the larvae grow inside your healthy puppy, migrating through his tissues into the bloodstream and eventually into his heart. Preventative medications are available and may be recommended by your vet, depending on the area that you live in. However, they must never be given to a dog who is already infected with adult worms. Always consult your veterinarian before starting any preventative treatment for heartworms.

- **Hookworms:** Diarrhoea, vomiting, and life-threatening anaemia are a few serious health problems associated with this parasite. Hookworms attach to the lining of your puppy's intestine, feeding on his oxygen-carrying blood. Puppies often become infected through their mother. Good sanitary practices will help prevent the spread of hookworms. That's why it is important to pick up faecal material daily.

- **Roundworms:** Roundworms live in a dog's small intestine and absorb nutrients, interfere with digestion, and can damage the lining of your puppy's intestine. Roundworms are resistant to environmental

## Eradicating Fleas

- Clean anything and everything your puppy has come in contact with.
- Wash all dog beds and blankets, and mop up floors.
- Vacuum all carpets, rugs, furniture, and the inside of your car. Immediately dispose of vacuum bags because eggs can hatch in them.
- Remove dense vegetation near your home, garden, or kennel area—these spaces offer a damp microenvironment that fleas love and in which they thrive.
- Treat your puppy and any other household pets who can serve as hosts, such as other dogs, cats, and ferrets.

conditions and most common disinfectants. They can adhere to your puppy's skin, hair, and paws, so good hygiene and strict sanitation practices are essential to minimise further contamination. Roundworms can live for months or even years once they get into the soil.

- **Tapeworms:** Although not normally life-threatening, tapeworms are a problem because they live in your puppy's gut, attach to the wall of the intestine, and absorb nutrients. Flea and lice control are essential, otherwise your puppy will continue to reinfest himself.

- **Whipworms:** Whipworms live in the large intestine, where they feed on blood. Whipworms can live in the moist soil for years, so dogs who bury their bones or dig in the dirt or eat grass can pick up eggs. To help reduce or prevent contamination, faecal matter must be picked up daily, and kennel or dog run areas must be cleaned thoroughly.

## General Illnesses

Common health problems are found in most breeds of dogs, and educating yourself about what can go wrong is the best defence when it comes to keeping your puppy happy and healthy well into his senior years.

Let's take a look at some of the most common canine diseases that can affect your puppy.

## Allergies

Flea-bite allergies, food allergies, and inhalant allergies are three of the more common allergies you are likely to see in dogs.

### Flea Bite Dermatitis

Also known as *bite hypersensitivity*, one bite from this tiny, nearly invisible pest can make your dog's life (and yours!) miserable. Flea allergy dermatitis tends to be most prevalent during the summer and fall, when fleas are most rampant and annoying. Dogs with flea allergies—meaning dogs who are hypersensitive to flea bites—may itch over their entire bodies, experience generalised hair loss, and develop red, inflamed skin and hot spots.

Frequently restless and uncomfortable, dogs may spend a great deal of time scratching, digging, licking, and chewing at their skin. Diagnosis consists of observing visual signs, as well as the presence of fleas and, in many cases, intradermal skin testing.

Treatments can be multifaceted, but prevention—preventing fleas from biting your dog—is the primary treatment. Others include over-the-counter hypoallergenic or colloidal oatmeal-type shampoos to remove allergens, and

*Preventative medications are available for many internal parasites.*

topical anti-itch creams to soothe the skin. Fatty acid supplements, such as omega-3 and omega-6 (found in flaxseed and fish oils) are proving helpful in reducing the amount and effects of the histamine that your dog's body produces. These histamines cause the inflammation and itch. In some cases, your veterinarian may prescribe something to help reduce itching.

## Food Allergies

Like humans, dogs can also be allergic to foods, including beef, chicken, dairy products, wheat, maize, and soy—not surprisingly, the most common ingredients in dog food! Symptoms are similar to those of atopic dermatitis—scratching, itching, chewing, hair loss, and red, inflamed, or irritated skin—and that can make diagnosing food allergies a bit tricky. Food trials—feeding a very specific diet for twelve weeks—are the most effective method of providing a definitive diagnosis. Treatment is pretty straightforward and requires owners to eliminate the offending food source from their dog's diet by feeding either a special commercially prepared diet or a homemade diet.

## Inhalant Allergies

Inhalant allergies are caused by a genetic predisposition and hypersensitivity to environmental allergens, such as dust mites, mould, spores, grass, and weed pollen. Exposure to these allergens—usually when pollen activity is high—triggers your dog's immune system, causing itchy and inflamed skin. Chewing,

# Life-Threatening Symptoms

If your puppy has any of these symptoms, seek medical assistance right away:

- Bleeding that is heavy or can't be stopped
- Breathing that is difficult or laboured, or no breathing at all
- Collapse, coma, depression, extreme lethargy, or unconsciousness
- Diarrhoea that is uncontrolled or bloody, or stools that are black and tarry
- Gums that are bluish or white
- Pain
- Seizures
- Temperature over 105°F (41°C). (The average body temperature for a dog is 101.5°F [38.6°C]).
- Vomiting (especially uncontrolled vomiting)
- Teeth that are broken, bleeding, or loose

digging, scratching, and biting at the skin are primary symptoms, which can cause secondary skin infections. No definitive atopic dermatitis test exists, so veterinarians use a process of elimination. They first look at the dog's history and symptoms, then rule out other conditions, such as food allergies, flea infestation, parasites, and

# Breed-specific Illnesses

An important part of responsible dog ownership is understanding what can go wrong before anything does go wrong. Hopefully your puppy will grow into an adult dog who is happy and healthy. However, some breeds are more prone or predisposed to specific illnesses. Some Rottweilers, for example, carry the subaortic stenosis (SAS) gene, which causes a specific heart problem. Hip dysplasia is more common in medium- to large-breed dogs than in toy breeds. Some herding breeds, such as Australian Shepherds, Collies, and Shetland Sheepdogs, as well as a few other breeds, are more sensitive to certain drugs, such as ivermectin (an antiparasitic drug) and Imodium (an over-the-counter anti-diarrhoea agent) that result in adverse reactions requiring an extended hospital stay—these drugs may even cause death.

Again, that's not to say your puppy will develop a specific medical condition. Most reputable breeders manage their breeding programmes with an eye on eliminating or preventing breed-specific illnesses. However, by understanding which diseases are most likely to affect your breed, you are more likely to recognise when something is amiss. Education is the key, and timely veterinary treatment can mean the difference between a happy, healthy puppy and a tearful ending.

mange, which have similar symptoms. Although incurable, atopic dermatitis can often be controlled through immunotherapy and medications, such as antihistamines or steroids. Reducing your dog's exposure to triggering allergens, combined with the use of household filters, hypoallergenic shampoos, topical anti-itch creams, and omega-3 and omega-6 supplements can help when combined with veterinary treatment.

## Dental Problems

Dogs do just about everything with their mouths, from exploring their environment to eating and drinking to chewing on rocks, sticks, and any number of human-offensive delicacies. While dogs don't get cavities, they do experience many painful dental problems similar to humans, such as broken teeth, gingivitis, and periodontal disease.

## Fractured Teeth

Dogs can break their teeth in any number of ways and on any number of objects, such as chewing on rocks, chain link enclosures, and bones that are too hard. Car accidents, dog fights, or a fall from a car window or balcony can also lead to broken teeth. Working dogs occasionally fracture their teeth while herding.

Sometimes you can see a broken

tooth, especially a canine or incisor. Other times, you may notice clues, such as bleeding or pain when you touch your dog's jaw or a specific tooth. Some dogs have difficulty eating, or they may not drink cold water. Some breeds are very stoic and may not show symptoms of pain even when they are experiencing it. In many cases, your veterinarian may notice a broken tooth during a dental examination or routine visit.

Fractured teeth can create a great deal of pain for your dog, especially if the broken tooth exposes the pulp—the soft inner portion of the tooth containing the blood vessels and tissues. If left untreated, bacteria can lodge in the damaged tissue and cause countless problems ranging from inflammation to abscesses. Treatment depends on which parts of the tooth are broken. Serious breaks may require extraction or reconstructive surgery not unlike people receive, such as root canals and crowns.

## Gingivitis and Periodontal Disease

Did you know you should be brushing your puppy's teeth everyday? It's true. Like people, dogs develop tartar on their teeth when minerals and saliva combine with plaque. As tartar accumulates, it irritates your dog's gums and causes an inflammatory condition called *gingivitis*. Look closely at your dog's teeth—do you see a yellowish-brown crust forming and the reddening of

gums next to the teeth? If so, that's tartar, and a trip to the veterinarian's should be in his immediate future. If left untreated, gingivitis will develop into periodontal disease, which is irreversible—and painful. Imagine living with a toothache for years!

If the tartar is not removed, the cycle continues to repeat itself. Tartar builds up under the gums, causing them to separate from the teeth, causing even larger pockets, where more debris can collect. These pockets encourage even more bacterial growth and, when left untreated, the tissue and bones that support the teeth erode, causing pain and eventual tooth loss. In advanced stages of periodontal disease, bacteria can enter the bloodstream, causing secondary infections that can damage your dog's heart, liver, and kidneys.

Bad breath, tartar accumulation, and

*Chewing on inappropriate items can damage your puppy's teeth.*

red, swollen gums are the most visible indications of trouble. Drooling or a sensitivity to brushing or touching the gums, difficulty chewing or eating, irritability, or depression are additional symptoms.

Treatment may include difficult and extensive surgeries, depending on the condition's severity. However, prevention is as simple as home care, including routine inspections of your dog's mouth, daily brushing, dental chew toys, a diet that includes a balanced premium food, and regular visits to the veterinarian's surgery for oral examinations and professional teeth cleaning.

## Diarrhoea

If your puppy has diarrhoea, you should err on the side of caution and seek veterinary assistance right away. Any number of serious illnesses, such as parvovirus, coronavirus, salmonella, parasites, or several small-intestine diseases, can be life-threatening situations.

That said, puppies can get diarrhoea for any number of other reasons including if you change his normal food from one brand to another too quickly or if there is a change in water while travelling. (That's why it's important to carry your own water or purchase bottled water.) Dirty feeding bowls, stress, and allergies can also cause diarrhoea. If the diarrhoea is slight, and your dog has no other symptoms, it may be nothing more than minor gastric upset. A bland diet of cooked white rice and boiled chicken or extra lean mince browned in a pan with any excess grease removed may correct the problem. Over-the-counter anti-diarrhoeal medications may also help. However, some breeds, such as Australian Shepherds, Shetland Sheepdogs, long-haired Whippets, English Sheepdogs, and German Shepherds, may have adverse and life-threatening reactions to these medications. Always consult your veterinarian before giving any human medications to your puppy.

## Vomiting

As with diarrhoea, if your puppy is vomiting, it is prudent to seek veterinary assistance, because vomiting can be a symptom of stomach, intestinal, kidney, liver, and other diseases.

That said, dogs vomit occasionally, and they can do so with little

62

*Keep your puppy's mouth healthy by brushing his teeth.*

## First-Aid Kit

If you have a puppy—or kids!—you should have a first-aid kit for both because both have the uncanny ability to get into anything and everything when you least expect it. Of course, if your puppy is sick or injured, always err on the side of caution and seek veterinary assistance.

Your doggy first-aid kit should contain the following basic ingredients:

- Activated charcoal
- Alcohol or alcohol prep pads
- Anti-diarrhoea medicine
- Eye wash or saline solution
- Eye ointment
- Gauze rolls and gauze pads
- Gloves
- Hydrogen peroxide
- Important telephone numbers
- Iodine
- Lubricant
- Muzzle
- Pen and paper
- Rehydrating solution
- Scissors
- Styptic pencil
- Thermometer
- Towels, blanket, or old sheet
- Tweezers

discomfort. Excitability, drinking too much water too fast (especially after exercise), gulping their food, or after they've eaten grass are a few of the many reasons dogs may vomit. If your puppy appears to be healthy, a single vomiting incident should not send you rushing to the vet. It may be nothing more than a simple upset stomach. If the problem persists, or if your puppy has other symptoms, such as diarrhoea, stomach bloating, listlessness, laboured breathing, pain, or you see blood in the vomit or abnormal material, seek immediate veterinary assistance. And don't forget to take a sample of the vomit with you, because it can help the veterinarian with the diagnosis.

## Emergencies and First Aid

Puppies have the uncanny ability to get into anything and everything—usually at the most inopportune and unexpected times! If your puppy is sick or injured, always err on the side of caution and contact your veterinarian or 24-hour emergency clinic right away. Many minor situations, such as scrapes, nicks, abrasions, or a bout of diarrhoea, can be successfully treated at home, coupled with a "wait and see" attitude. It is important, however, that you be able to recognise the difference between a minor situation and a life-threatening medical emergency.

# Chapter 6

# Train Me!

Training your puppy is fun! It's also an important and necessary part of puppy ownership because it helps to build a strong human–canine bond, which is important if you want your puppy to grow into a well-behaved adult. Your puppy's cuddly good looks and puppy antics make him irresistible—but don't let his appearance deceive you. At an early age, he quickly can learn to manipulate you, so you must start to instil positive behaviours, basic obedience commands, and household rules right away.

Puppies who do not have a solid foundation of canine manners and obedience skills quickly grow into unruly hooligans. Basic obedience moves, such as sit, down, come, and walking on lead, will provide your puppy with a set of commands he understands, thereby making your life and his more enjoyable.

As your puppy grows bigger and bolder and ventures through canine adolescence—a stage similar to raising teenagers—your training plans and good intentions may fall by the wayside when he chooses to ignore your commands, bolts out doors, jumps on people, or swipes food off the kitchen counter. The good news is that most of these problems are entirely predictable. Rest assured: Your puppy is not the first nor will he be the last to test his boundaries. However, armed with a good game plan and a bit of knowledge, many of these problems are entirely preventable. At the very least, you can keep them from escalating into major stumbling blocks that can preclude a long and mutually respectful human-canine relationship.

## Why Dogs Do What They Do

Understanding why puppies do what they do will greatly increase your chance of success and help expedite the training process. Canine genetics and animal behaviour are elementary—if you have a Ph.D.! Otherwise, they are complicated and exhausting topics that go well beyond the scope of this book. In the simplest of terms—and

## Why the Training Fuss?

Exposing your puppy to basic obedience commands and teaching him to respond reliably and quickly to your commands as he grows and matures makes him much easier and enjoyable to live with. No doubt his life is more pleasurable because, as a well-behaved dog, he is more likely to be incorporated into the family environment, rather than relegated to the isolation of the back garden.

without delving too deeply into the complexities of canine genetics—it is safe to say that dogs do what they do for two reasons: inherited behaviours and acquired behaviours.

## Inherited Behaviours

While not always the traits you bargained for, inherited behaviours are part and parcel of your puppy's complete package. Also known as genetic predispositions, they are the traits that Mother Nature genetically programmed into your dog. For example, Huskies were originally bred as endurance sled dogs. Their inherent desire to run—and run and run and run—makes it nearly impossible for the average owner to allow them off lead under any circumstances. Terriers are feisty, energetic dogs whose ancestors were bred to hunt and kill vermin. Leaving a terrier unattended in your garden and expecting him not to dig is wishful thinking. Herding dogs, such as Border Collies, are high-energy, high-drive dogs that have been genetically programmed over hundreds of years to herd livestock. They take great pleasure in attacking moving objects and chasing fleeing kids on bicycles.

By understanding the history and origin of your breed—the job for which he was originally bred—you will have a better understanding of your puppy's predispositions. You can then learn to work within the confines of your chosen breed by designing a training programme that best suits your puppy's individual and inherited characteristics.

## Acquired Behaviours

Acquired behaviours are learned behaviours. Behaviours that your puppy has learned—be they good or bad, desired or undesired—since the day he was born. Swiping food off the counter, refusing to come when called, peeing from one end of the house to the other, bolting out the front door, and committing heinous crimes against your personal property are all acquired behaviours. A ten-week-old Border Collie who learns to have fun chasing young children and nipping

**67**

*Understanding your breed's inherited traits can make training easier—this Aussie pup has herding in his blood!*

their trouser legs will see no harm in doing this as a 50-pound (23 kg) adult dog. An adorable Poodle puppy who is mollycoddled every time he whines or barks will grow into an adult Poodle who barks and whines whenever he wants attention.

That said, acquired behaviours can be positive, too. If you call your six-month-old Labrador Retriever and he tears over to you with his head and ears up and his tail wagging—that too is an acquired behaviour; your puppy has learned to come when he is called. If you train your puppy to respect you, you won't end up with a dog who begs, steals food, or bolts out doors.

## Positive Training

Dogs learn through repetition and consistency. If each and every time your puppy comes to you he is rewarded with a "Good Boy!" and a tasty tidbit of food, chances are high that he will grow into an adult dog who thinks coming to you is fun and highly rewarding. This is the essence of positive motivation/reinforcement. Simply put, if a behaviour has a favourable response, the more likely a puppy is to repeat the behaviour. A puppy learns to repeat a behaviour, such as *sit, down*, or *come*, to receive a reward, be it a tasty tidbit of food, a toy, or a kiss on the nose—or a combination of all three.

If, on the other hand, you call your puppy to you and he comes running to

you willingly and then you scold him for chewing your shoe or urinating on the rug, you are teaching him to avoid you when you say the word "come." In the dog's mind he is thinking, "The last time I came running when you called, you yelled at me, so I don't think I'll do that again."

Positive training isn't just about randomly doling out tasty tidbits. You are not a biscuit dispenser for every little thing your puppy does. You must pay attention to what behaviours you are reinforcing. For example, if your puppy is barking and you tell him, "It's okay, honey. Mummy loves you," the dog thinks he is being rewarded for barking. He thinks, "When I bark, my mum tells me it's okay. So I should keep barking." You communicated

*By keeping training positive, you'll increase the bond between you and your puppy.*

exactly the opposite of what you wanted. Try to look at what you are saying, and how you are saying it, from your puppy's point of view.

## Social Development: Important

### TIMES IN YOUR PUPPY'S LIFE

Certain periods in a puppy's life are critical to his social development. What happens within these individual stages has an enormous and significant impact on a puppy's future behaviour as an adult dog. For example, from

*Socialising your puppy with other dogs can help him grow confident.*

birth to three weeks, your puppy is helpless. His canine mother provides his nourishment, security, and warmth. Around four weeks of age, he still needs his canine mum, but he's also a bit stronger and will try to play with his littermates. From five to seven weeks of age, puppies grow rapidly, becoming more coordinated. Wrestling and playing with their littermates, they learn how to interact and get along with other dogs. The dam will begin disciplining her puppies, too, should they bite too hard or get out of line.

Between eight and sixteen weeks is an important socialisation period for your puppy. There is much he needs to learn, and what happens during this timeframe has a significant impact on his behaviour as an adult. You must use your time wisely to maximise this small window of opportunity. Squandering your opportunities during this time means that you run the risk

**69**

## Don't Miss Out

If possible, avoid scheduling holidays or extended trips out of town while your puppy is between eight and sixteen weeks of age—unless, of course, you plan to take him with you. Boarding him in a kennel or leaving him in the care of friends or relatives during this time puts your puppy at a serious disadvantage later in life. You will have missed a prime opportunity to shape his future character and instil all the behaviours you want your puppy to possess as an adult dog.

of having your puppy develop bad habits that are difficult, if not impossible, to correct later in life.

Exposing your puppy to positive experiences during the socialisation period, such as handling, grooming, and different sights and sounds, means he stands a better chance of developing the socialisation skills and coping mechanisms necessary to grow into a mentally sound and confident adult dog. Older puppies who have not been adequately or properly socialised during these periods tend to be more cautious. They generally grow up shy, fearful, and frequently nervous. As an adult dog, they find it difficult, if not impossible, to cope with new experiences.

Socialisation is the single most important process in a puppy's life. Breeders and owners owe it to their puppies to take advantage of this

critical period to maximise their future, foster their zany personalities, and instil desired behaviours. How much time and energy you invest during this critical period directly impacts the future character of your puppy.

## Your Role Starts Early

Your job begins the day you bring your puppy home. You must protect him from traumatic or bad experiences, while simultaneously instilling desired behaviours, such as coming when called and toileting outdoors. Fostering his upbeat personality and providing him with every opportunity to grow into a well-adjusted, mentally confident adult dog is the essence of socialisation.

The importance of maximising your opportunities during this critical period cannot be overly stressed. Puppies mature faster than humans. On the average, humans take about eighteen years to reach maturity, while puppies take about one to one-and-a-half years—depending on the breed. Your puppy will be eight weeks old for exactly seven days. The same goes for being nine, ten, eleven, and twelve weeks old. While one week may seem insignificant in the lifespan of a child, it represents a significant portion of your puppy's puppyhood. Once those seven days have passed, they can never be recaptured.

## Socialising Your Puppy

Chances are good that your puppy received at least one puppy shot before leaving the breeder's home. However, prudence dictates consulting your veterinarian about any necessary puppy vaccinations before taking your puppy outdoors and around other animals.

Then, in a fun, safe, and stress-free environment, begin exposing your puppy to anything and everything he is likely to encounter as an adult dog, such as babies in pushchairs, toddlers, teenagers, and women in floppy hats. Expose him to other dogs, cats, horses, goats, sheep, and so forth, as well as the clapping of hands, the jingling of keys, and the clatter of dog bowls. Let him explore different surfaces, such as grass, cement, gravel, tile, carpet, linoleum, sand, and dirt. City pavements, pastures, stairs, paper bags blowing in the wind, wind chimes, and honking horns should also be included in his socialisation agenda.

Let your puppy play in and around empty boxes, tunnels, and buckets. Allow him to investigate trees, rocks, bushes, branches, leaves, and fallen fruit. Fun rides in the car and walks in the park are excellent ways to socialise your puppy. Visits to the post office, flower shop, veterinarian's surgery, and outdoor cafe should be on your must-do list for puppy treats and kisses.

Socialisation is all about exposing your puppy to positive experiences, while simultaneously protecting him from harmful or fearful situations. Keep a watch on your puppy's reactions to different situations. Watch his eyes, tail, and body posture. By understanding your puppy's body language, you can evaluate and adjust the situation accordingly. For example, if your puppy is fearful while playing with other

*Puppies should be exposed to gentle, respectful children.*

larger, rambunctious puppies, avoid coddling or reinforcing the fear. Rather, modify or restrict the exposure to one or several less rambunctious puppies similar in size. Noisy, rambunctious children can be equally traumatic for puppies who were raised in a childless environment. Restrict or modify his environment to one or two quiet, well-behaved children until your puppy's confidence can handle more. When your puppy is brave, praise and reinforce him for being brave and inquisitive. "Good puppy!" or "Look at you. Aren't you brave!"

If you do nothing else for your puppy, you owe it to him to make the time to properly and adequately socialise him during this critical life stage. Yes, it's time consuming, but it is a necessary and obligatory investment when you choose to raise a puppy. His future well-being depends on how much you do—or fail to do—during this critical period.

## Puppy Classes

Puppy classes can offer wonderful socialisation opportunities for you and your puppy. Most classes are designed for puppies between two and five months of age and are ideal environments for exposing and socialising your puppy to the many things he will encounter in his adult life—including other dogs, people, boxes, chairs, stairs, rubbish bins, strange noises, kids, toys, and so forth. Puppy classes also help your puppy continue to expand on his knowledge

*Puppy Classes can offer a great socialisation opportunity for your puppy.*

## Challenging the Rules

Between twelve and sixteen weeks of age, your puppy will be bigger, bolder, and more confident. He won't need you quite as much as he used to, and he may choose to ignore your commands. He is checking to see if the household rules will be enforced. This is a critical juncture in the human–canine relationship. You mustn't become complacent. Make sure that everyone in the household is enforcing household rules consistently.

of canine communication and social skills that he learned from his mother and while interacting with his littermates.

Puppy classes should not be a free-for-all, where puppies play on their own while their owners socialise on the sidelines. Puppies have limited attention spans and are easily distracted. Therefore, a well-structured puppy class should include equal parts play and learning that exposes the pups, in a fun and stress-free environment, to basic obedience skills, such as fun puppy recall games, sit, down, and name recognition. You should learn how to read your puppy's body language, how to train him, and how to recognise problems early on, before they become annoying habits that are difficult to break.

### Finding the Right Puppy Class

Puppy class curriculum, prices, and training methods vary from trainer to trainer. To find the right trainer and class for you and your puppy:

- Ask your veterinarian, breeder, dog groomer, or dog-owning friends for referrals. Word-of-mouth is a great tool for uncovering talented and knowledgeable trainers, and avoiding problem ones.

- Contact professional organisations that certify or recommend trainers, such as the Association of Pet Dog Trainers.

- Attend the classes of several trainers to observe their personalities, training techniques, and facilities.

- Look for trainers who utilise positive motivation, as well as focus on rewarding what your puppy does right rather than punishing what he does wrong.

- Does the trainer recognise that puppies are individuals? Is he or she familiar with your breed? Are the same training methods imposed on all the puppies, regardless of their breed and mental maturity?

- Puppies learn best in a low-risk, stress-free environment. Look for classes that are structured, run smoothly, and emphasise fun.

- Do the facilities provide a safe learning environment for you and your puppy? Are they well lit, with matted floors and eight to ten

Train Me!

puppies per class?

- Are the puppies separated—small puppies from large, young puppies from juniors, the rambunctious from the shy?

- Trust your instincts. Your puppy's safety and well-being are paramount. If you feel uncomfortable about the facility or trainer, find another puppy class.

*Safety is important for a puppy class.*

## Crate Training

Think of a crate as a training tool—not unlike a lead, collar, or tasty tidbit. Many owners look upon a crate as cruel or inhumane. "I would never put my dog in a cage!" they exclaim. When viewed from a dog's point of view, a crate isn't a cage but rather an extension of his natural desire to seek a safe, enclosed environment. Years ago, before dogs became domesticated pets, they sought safe, enclosed areas for security and protection. A crate replicates or mimics that safe, protected environment. Puppies, especially very young puppies, tire quickly and need a lot of sleep during the day. A crate placed in a quiet corner of your living room or kitchen will satisfy your dog's natural instinct to seek a safe, secure environment. A place he can get away from the poking, prodding fingers of boisterous children. A place all his own, to curl up in when he is tired.

Equally important, a crate provides a safe environment for your puppy when you cannot watch him like a hawk, such as when you are showering, paying bills, working on the computer, or talking on the telephone. Confining your puppy in a crate during these times puts him in a position where he cannot develop bad habits or inadvertently get himself into trouble by chewing indiscriminately or peeing on your new carpeting.

Crates are ideal for travelling, too. A crated dog will not distract you from your driving responsibilities, teethe on your leather seats, chew on your designer purse, ransack the groceries, eat your mobile phone.

Many hotels, as well as family and friends, are more receptive to dogs when they are crate-trained. As your puppy grows and matures, the crate will continue to be his den and safe place for eating, sleeping, and retreating from the often chaotic and noisy world of humans.

## How to Crate Train Your Puppy

Most puppies quickly learn to love their crate when it is associated with good things, such as feeding time, yummy treats, security, and sleep. With any luck, the breeder will have started some crate training. To maximise the crate training process, make the crate attractive to your puppy by placing a cosy crate pad, old blanket, or rug, and a few of his favourite chew toys inside the crate. Remember, puppies love to chew, so choose toys and bedding that do not present a potential choking hazard. Leave the crate door open and allow your puppy to explore in and around the crate. When he goes inside the crate, praise him. "Good puppy!" or "Aren't you clever!" Reward him with a tasty tidbit while he is in the crate, but don't close or latch the door just yet.

For the reluctant puppy, encourage him by letting him see you toss a tasty tidbit of food inside the crate, preferably toward the back. Incorporate your kids in the training process by allowing them to be the designated biscuit throwers. When your puppy goes inside the crate to retrieve the food, praise him. "Good puppy!" You can also begin introducing a cue phase, such as "Go to your kennel" or "Kennel up" as he goes inside the crate. Leave the door closed for longer and longer periods of time.

Feed your puppy his meals inside the crate. With any luck, he will charge right in after his food. If not, place his food bowl inside the crate, close to the opening, but leave the door open. Be patient, progress in small steps, and remember to reward positive behaviour. If your puppy whines or cries, avoid reinforcing the behaviour by letting him out. Wait for him to be quiet for a few seconds before opening the door.

As your puppy becomes more comfortable with the crate, gradually increase the time he spends there. Never confine him for longer than one or two hours at a time—except at night when he is sleeping.

*A soft bed looks fun for your puppy, but you should also supply him with a crate—a useful tool for housetraining.*

## Don't Abuse the Crate

A crate, like any other training tool, has the potential to be abused. A crate is not intended for 24-hour confinement. Your puppy should live with you and not in his crate. Never use a crate as a form of punishment. If used properly, a crate becomes a place your puppy loves, thereby making your life—and his— more enjoyable.

## Housetraining

Housetraining is a relatively simple and painless process, yet it's the one aspect of puppy rearing that causes owners a great deal of angst. Good planning and preparation and your unwavering commitment to the situation are the keys to success.

Increasing your chances of success while minimising accidents means providing your puppy with a regular schedule of eating, sleeping, and toileting. What goes in on a regular basis comes out on a regular basis. Dogs are creatures of habit, and your puppy will have an easier time adjusting to his new household and a housetraining schedule if you establish some order and routine to his life.

## Crate or Paper Training?

Crate training is by far the most efficient method of housetraining. Remember, if your puppy were born

in the wild, he would live in a cave or den, and most den animals have an instinctive desire to keep their dens clean. As a result, they tend to avoid relieving themselves in their den. A crate serves as your puppy's den, and a dog's deep-seated instinct to keep his den clean provides the foundation of housetraining via use of a crate. If you take advantage of this natural instinct, you reduce the chance of accidents. As your puppy matures, you gradually teach him to hold his bladder for longer periods of time.

Paper training, on the other hand, is an older yet still utilised method of training. It works well for people with tiny dogs or for those who live in high-rise flats and can't run down 30 floors every hour or whenever their puppy looks like he needs to relieve himself. The drawback is that once you allow your puppy to toilet indoors—even on paper—it creates the behaviour of toileting in the house, which can create an entirely new set of problems down the road. Eventually, at some point in time, you need to backtrack and train your puppy to relieve himself outdoors.

## How to Housetrain Your Puppy

Puppies have very little or no bladder control until around five months of age. Accepting this fact of puppyhood is the first step in any successful housetraining programme. Puppies also mature at different rates, so your puppy's control may develop earlier or later. Your seven- or eight-week-old puppy is equivalent to a four- or six-month-old human baby. You would not expect a young baby to control his bladder, and it is unfair to ask your puppy to exercise control he does not have.

As he matures, he will gradually learn to hold his bladder for longer periods. Puppies are also most active during the day—running, jumping, training, playing, exploring, and just being a puppy. Because of their limited bladder size and lack of control, they are going to need to relieve themselves many, many times throughout the day. During the night, however, puppies are usually exhausted from their busy day. They are more relaxed at this time, so most can sleep between five and eight hours without having to toilet. If your puppy wakes you up in the middle of the night or in the early morning because he needs to go, it is always better to get up with him. The fewer accidents he has in his crate, the less stressful the process will be. Although it may seem forever, it won't be long before he can hold on all night.

### When to Take Your Puppy Out

Until your puppy begins developing some reliable bladder control, which can be anywhere from five to twelve months, depending on your puppy's breed, as well as your commitment and diligence, you must take your puppy outdoors frequently. Your 100 percent commitment to a regular schedule means your puppy will learn quicker, and that means fewer accidents in the house.

As a general guideline—to increase your chances of success while minimising accidents—take your

Paper training may be an option if you live in a flat.

puppy outdoors at the following times:

- First thing in the morning when he wakes up, and at least every hour throughout the day.
- About fifteen minutes after drinking water.
- About thirty minutes after eating.
- Immediately after waking from a nap.
- Every time you arrive home.
- Anytime you take him out of his crate.
- Anytime he shows signs of having to go.
- Last thing at night.

This guideline is for young puppies, which, of course, are unique and individual. You may need to tweak or adjust this schedule to fit your puppy's particular needs.

## When You're Outside

While outside, watch your puppy closely to be sure he relieves himself. It may take a few minutes, so be patient. When your puppy has finished doing his business, calmly praise: "Good toilet" or "Good puppy." Once you have seen your puppy relieve himself outdoors, you can allow him supervised play indoors. If you take your puppy outdoors and he gets sidetracked playing or sniffing bugs and does not relieve himself, you must put him back in his crate for five or ten minutes and then repeat the aforementioned

*Don't punish your puppy for housetraining mistakes.*

steps. (If you are not using a crate, keep your puppy where you can watch him like a hawk for those five or ten minutes). Do this as many times as necessary until your puppy relieves himself outdoors. Never assume your puppy has done his business. You must see him empty his bladder or bowels. Here's the reason why: If your puppy gets distracted outdoors and forgets to toilet and then you bring him back indoors and give him free run of the house—guess where he's going to toilet when he's no longer distracted and has a sudden urge to go? The odds are sky high that he will toilet on your carpet.

You need to repeat this routine many, many times throughout the day and again just before you go to bed. No one said raising a puppy was all fun and no work! Housetraining a puppy is a time-consuming endeavour, but time invested at this stage will make your life easier in the long run.

## Basic Obedience

Basic obedience skills provide your puppy with a set of commands he understands, thereby making your life and his more enjoyable. Trying to restrain a 50-pound (23 kg) dog who wants to zig when you want to zag is enough to make you wish you had bought a cat.

Equally important, puppies have limited attention spans and are easily distracted by kids playing, birds singing, horses whinnying, and so forth. Expecting your puppy to ignore distractions and focus entirely on you is unreasonable. Always set your puppy up to succeed by starting his training in a familiar environment that has a limited amount of distractions, such as your living room or back garden.

## Name Recognition

Every puppy must know his name, and teaching it is relatively easy. Start with a pocket full of tasty treats. Stand or kneel close to your puppy, and say his name in a fun, happy voice. When he looks at you, reward him with verbal praise, "Good boy!" and a tasty tidbit. Practice this several times a day, and it won't be long before he knows his name.

## Sit

Think of the many situations in which your puppy will need to know how

## Warning Signs

The housetraining process runs amok when owners think their puppy is housetrained when it is only wishful thinking on their part. Some puppies are harder to housetrain than others and chances are your puppy will not be reliably housetrained until he is at least six months old.

Puppies between the ages of eight and ten weeks do not show signs of having to urinate. When they have to go, they go right away—often stopping to urinate in the middle of their play session. It is unrealistic to expect an eight-week-old puppy to stop what he is doing and tell you he needs to go outside. More often than not, your puppy will not realise he has to go until he is already going.  Around ten or twelve weeks of age, a puppy will start to exhibit signs—warning signals that he is about to urinate or defecate—by circling, making crying noises, sniffing the floor, arching his back, or standing by the door. This is where owners get over confident and think they are home free. These are signs that your puppy is learning, not that he is housetrained. You mustn't become complacent. Now more than ever you need to remain diligent and stick to the programme. Puppies are either housetrained or they aren't. Any wavering on your part will only set your puppy up for problems down the road.

*Using food as a reward is a great way to train your puppy.*

hips will automatically touch the ground. Give the *sit* command as your puppy's rear end hits the ground. Praise with "Good sit!" and reward with the treat— while your puppy is sitting.

Release your puppy with a release word, such as "Okay," play with him for a few seconds, and repeat the exercise three or four times in succession, three or four times a day.

to sit—at the vet's surgery, waiting to be fed, or sitting and waiting while you open any door. He will need to sit when you put his collar on or take it off, wipe his feet, when you want to check his coat for stickers or burs, or when you want to brush him or trim his nails.

Teaching the sit is relatively simple, and the guidelines are the same whether you are teaching a young puppy or an adult dog.

Start by showing your puppy a tidbit of food. Hold it close to and slightly above his nose.

Slowly move the treat in a slightly upward and backward direction toward his tail, keeping the treat directly above his nose. If your puppy's front feet come off the ground, the treat is too high. If he walks backwards, the treat is too far back or too low.

When done correctly, your puppy's

## Down

Down is an equally important and useful command. Your dog may need to lie down when the vet examines him, while you brush or scratch his tummy, or when you want to massage his sore muscles.

Begin by kneeling on the floor, so that you are at eye level with your puppy. With him standing in front of you, hold a tasty tidbit of food in one hand. While your puppy is sniffing the tidbit, move it toward the floor between his front paws. When done correctly, your puppy will plant his front feet and fold his body into the *down* position as he follows the food to the ground.

When your puppy is in the *down* position, reward him with the treat and calmly praise him with a "Good down." Release your puppy with a release word, such as "Okay," and repeat the exercise three or four times in succession, three or four times a day.

## Stay

The goal of this command is to teach your dog to stay in a specific position, such as in a *sit* or *down*, until you say it is okay to move. It is useful in a variety of situations, such as when you want to open the door without your dog bolting through it.

A word of caution: Never try to teach this exercise to a young puppy, say, eight, ten, or twelve weeks old. Most puppies are not emotionally mature enough to cope with this exercise until they are five or six months old. If this is the case with your puppy, do not force the issue. Simply wait until he is older and mentally mature enough to understand the exercise.

To teach *sit-stay* start with your puppy on a loose lead, sitting beside you. Tell your puppy "Sit" and "Stay." Watch your puppy closely for the slightest movement that may indicate he is about to stand up or lie down. Be proactive in your training by reminding your dog to stay before he moves. If you see any movement, repeat your *stay* command firmly but not harshly.

Once he has remained in position for a few seconds, praise him calmly and warmly with "Good stay" and a treat. Include calm, physical praise, such as gentle stroking—but not so enthusiastically that he gets excited and forgets the task at hand. Depending on your

puppy, he may or may not be able to accept physical praise. For some dogs, the anticipation of physical praise is too much to contain themselves.

Release with the word "Okay." (Releasing your dog first and then rewarding him teaches him the wrong association. He will think that he is being rewarded for moving. This can teach a puppy to anticipate the reward, thereby encouraging him to break the *stay* command.)

Do not be in a hurry to move away from your dog or have him hold the position for longer periods. Progress in five-second increments until your dog can remain sitting beside you for two or three minutes without moving. Gradually begin increasing the distance between you and your dog.

To teach the *down-stay*, begin with your dog in the *down* position, and tell him to stay. Then follow the

*Reward your puppy with a treat as soon as he performs the* sit *command.*

instructions for the *sit-stay*. To avoid confusing your puppy, always teach the *down-stay* and the *sit-stay* on different days.

## Come

This is one of the easiest exercises to teach. Honestly! But it does cause owners a great deal of angst. The goal is to teach your puppy to come to you reliably, willingly, and immediately—without hesitation—upon hearing the command. He must learn to come reliably even when in a wide range of situations, such as at the park, in an emergency, anytime he gets loose, and even when he's playing with his canine pals.

In the beginning, when your puppy is very young—as young as eight, ten, or twelve weeks of age—teach this behaviour using fun games and tasty rewards. Ideally, though, as your puppy grows into an adult dog, you want him to come to you because you are the centre of his universe and he wants to be with you—not just because you have treats.

*Keep your puppy close to you when you begin teaching* come. *Wave a favourite toy and say "come".*

## Start by Playing "Find Me"

Use an informal game like "Find me!" to being teaching the *come* in a positive, fun, and exciting manner. This game capitalises on a dog's natural chase instinct and is excellent for instilling the *come* command in young puppies.

Start with a pocket full of tasty tidbits. Rev your puppy up by showing him a yummy treat, and then toss the treat down the hallway or across the living room. As your puppy runs for the treat, you run in the opposite direction and hide behind a chair or door as you say his name enthusiastically: "Fido! Fido! Fido!"

When your puppy finds you, make a big fuss: Get on the floor, roll around, and lavish him with a potpourri of kisses and praise. "Good come!" or "Aren't you clever! You found your mummy!" Repeat the game several times throughout the day, but not so many times that your puppy becomes bored.

You can also play this game outdoors, but be sure to play in a fenced area to protect your puppy from harm or prevent him from running away. When you are outside in your garden with your puppy, and he stops to sniff the grass or explore a bug, duck behind a tree or bush, clap your hands, and say his name in an exciting tone of voice. When he finds you, reward him with verbal praise and a tasty tidbit. Your puppy need not sit before he gets a treat. If you insist that your puppy sit before getting his treat, you will not be rewarding the most important part of the exercise, which is coming to you.

A puppy who views *come* as a fun game is more likely to develop a reliable response to the command. If this behaviour continues throughout his puppyhood, and you remain excited and enthusiastic each and every time he comes to you, you will have a strong and positive response to the command as he matures into an adult dog.

*The Expert Knows*

## Set Your Puppy Up to Succeed

When teaching the Come command, call your puppy only when you are absolutely certain he will respond. If you call your puppy when he is excited about greeting his canine buddies, when a family member has just arrived home, or when he is eating his dinner, he will be too excited and distracted to respond to your command, and you will inadvertently be teaching him to ignore you. In the early stages, when your puppy is learning the Come command, wait until the excitement has subsided and then call him to you. If you must have your puppy during these times, it is better to go and get him rather than call him to you.

Train Me!

## When Not to Use Come

To develop a reliable come command, *come* must always, always, always be positive. There is no wiggle room. If you call your puppy to come, you must always praise and reward when he gets to you—even if moments before he urinated on the floor or chewed your leather heels. Never use the Come command for anything your puppy might dislike or to end playtime. When you call your puppy, do something silly with him when he gets to you, such as a quick game of tug, a fun trick, or reward him with a tasty tidbit, and then let him run off and play again. Owners run amok by calling their puppy only when it is time to go in his kennel or put his lead on to go home. In these situations, your puppy quickly learns that "Come" means the end of his freedom, and he is likely to avoid you the next time he is called.

## Walk on Lead

It is always easier to teach your puppy to walk on lead by starting on the left side (the traditional heel position) and sticking with it until he understands the exercise. Once he has mastered walking nicely on lead, you can allow him to walk on either side or in front of you.

Walking on lead should always be something fun that you and your puppy do together. His lead and collar should never be associated with a barrage of jerks, pulls, and nagging corrections.

To start, attach a lead (or thin long line) to his collar and allow him to drag it around. (Always teach this exercise on a buckle collar, *never* a choke chain.) When your puppy is happily dragging the lead, pick it up and start walking forward, encouraging him to walk close to your left side by talking sweetly to him and luring him with a tasty tidbit from your left hand, which should be in a position close to your trouser seam. When you have walked a few steps with your puppy on your left side, reward him with the tidbit of food. Remember to verbally praise and offer the food reward when he is close beside your left leg. This encourages him to remain in position.

The training tips in this chapter only touch the surface of what is possible with your puppy. Once he is socialised, crate-trained, housetrained, and knows the basic commands, there is no end to the fun that you can have together.

*When your puppy learns to walk nicely on his lead, outings will be fun for both of you!*

## Kids and Training

Most children love interacting with the family pet. After all, who can resist a cute and adorable puppy? Puppies and kids usually go well together because they are equally energetic and inquisitive. However, kids must learn how to properly interact with a puppy, and you can maximise the situation while enhancing the human–canine bond by including your children in the training process.

How much responsibility you give your children in any part of life, including the responsibility of training and caring for a puppy, depends on their individual maturity level. Toddlers, for example, are not going to understand a long, wordy explanation about how to pet a dog. However, you can physically show a two-year-old how to pet a puppy by putting his hand in yours and petting the puppy together. Young children, say, four, five, or six years old, can help you "train" by helping you hold the lead while you take the puppy for a walk. You and your child can sit on the floor with your puppy and dole out plenty of calm pats, praise, and yummy treats. This helps both puppy and child form positive associations about being in each other's company. Older children, say, seven to ten years of age, can play the puppy recall game by sitting on the ground and calling the puppy between the two of you, and rewarding the puppy with yummy treats and plenty of praise. Under your supervision, they can help teach the puppy to sit and down, and they can keep track of when your puppy relieves himself, and sound the alarm when it is time to take him outside again. Some trainers allow children—around ten years of age and older—to handle a puppy in puppy class, depending on the child's maturity, the size and breed of the dog, and the puppy's activity level.

Teach your children to become skilled at reading canine body language by discussing dog behaviours you observe on television, in movies, in book or magazines, or at the park. For example, point out what a dog is doing on television. Is his tail up? Is he growling? Cowering? Confident? Excited? Worried? Playful? Make a fun game out of identifying what the dog's body language says, and why.

# Help Me!

# Solving Puppy Problems

Despite your puppy's irresistibly good looks and puppy antics, inevitably there will be times when he refuses to come when called, tracks mud through the house, and embarrasses you in front of your neighbours and in-laws. In a perfect world, your puppy would never get into trouble. In the real world, it is unrealistic to expect your puppy to grow into an adult dog without developing an annoying habit or two.

Keep in mind that most of these annoying "problems"—such as digging, barking, and chewing—are natural behaviours for your puppy. However, if left unchecked, these natural behaviours often turn into annoying problems for owners.

As guardian of your puppy, it is your job to teach him which behaviours are acceptable and which are not. But how do you keep your puppy out of the doghouse? First, it's important to realise that annoying or offensive behaviours do not appear suddenly. Your puppy does not lie around all day dreaming up ways to annoy you. "Tomorrow I'll shred the sofa. That'll show her who wears the trousers in this family!" A dog's brain is not hardwired to be vindictive. If he's committing heinous crimes against your personal property, chances are he is not being properly supervised.

Equally important, your puppy will not magically outgrow a barking, chewing, or peeing problem—or any problem for that matter. A puppy who digs holes in your garden will not suddenly stop digging, regardless of how much you hope he will. If you do not want your puppy jumping on you, ransacking the rubbish, or digging in your herb garden, you must modify his environment so that he is not put in a position where he can get himself into trouble.

If your puppy has already developed some bad habits and is well on his way to wearing out his welcome, it's not too late to get him out of the doghouse and back into your good graces.

## Barking (Excessively)

Some dogs—depending on the breed—are noisier than others. Often, barking is part and parcel of a breed's history. For example, many terriers—Silky Terrier, Yorkshire Terrier, Miniature Pinscher, Wire Fox Terrier, West Highland Terrier, Smooth Fox Terrier, to name a few—love to bark. Shelties are notorious for barking, and many of the small-breed dogs—Toy Poodle, Maltese, Chihuahua—also love to vocalise. That said, even those breeds without a propensity for noise can become noisy dogs if encouraged to bark or left to their own devices. If you have a noisy puppy, you'll want to curb any unnecessary barking from day one.

Dogs naturally bark or otherwise vocalise, and they

*Some puppies like to vocalise more than others.*

88

## Managing Him Indoors and Out

The best prevention against future barking problems is smart dog management:

- Never allow your puppy to be put in a situation where he is allowed to develop bad habits. Leaving him in the back garden unsupervised all day may inspire him to bark at constant stimuli, including other dogs barking, a cat on a fence, a bird overhead, leaves falling, neighbours coming and going, and life in general.

- A puppy housed indoors can also develop barking habits. If he sits on the furniture and stares out the living room window, he may be encouraged to bark at stimuli, such as neighbours, other dogs going for a walk, or kids on bicycles.

- If your dog barks during the excitement of play, halt the game immediately. When he stops barking, praise him with a "Good quiet!" or "Good boy!" Once you have regained control of the situation, begin playing again.

do so for various reasons and at various times, including when they get excited, when they are playing with other dogs, when the doorbell rings, and to greet you when you arrive home.

## Prevention

If you can quiet your puppy with a single command (or two!), you probably don't have much to worry about. Problems arise when your puppy is too hyped up to stop barking, and that's why curtailing this problem early on is a necessity. This includes never encouraging your puppy to bark. For example, when the doorbell rings, avoid asking your puppy, "What was that?" or "Let's go see!" This can excite your puppy and encourage him to bark. It may seem like a fun game when he is ten or twelve weeks old, but it is a difficult and annoying behaviour to

stop once it becomes ingrained.

Avoid soothing or coddling your puppy when he is barking, which inadvertently encourages the unwanted behaviour. If your puppy is barking, and you are telling him, "That's a good boy. It's okay. I love you," he will think that he is being reward for barking. In his mind he thinks, "When I bark, my mum says it's okay and praises me. I should keep barking."

Remember to always praise the behaviour you want, which is not barking. For example, the moment that your puppy stops barking, praise him with "Good quiet!" or "Good boy! That's what mummy wants." Fortunately, most barking problems can be avoided if you plan ahead, understand why your dog is barking, and have a clear picture of the behaviours that you will and will not accept.

## Chewing

Don't let your puppy's cute looks deceive you. Puppies—even the smallest ones—can be incredibly aggressive chewers, and it's a short leap from cute and adorable to one-dog demolition team. When left to their own devices, most puppies will gleefully shred magazines, cushion, shoes, electrical cables, table legs, plants, carpets, rugs, wallpaper, and anything else they can get their teeth on—and that's in the fifteen minutes it takes you to drive to the shop and back!

Puppies love to chew. It's a fact of life. They also *need* to chew, especially when they are teething, which varies from puppy to puppy. Most puppies undergo some form of continuous teething until they are about six to nine months of age. As their baby teeth fall out and their adult teeth erupt, it stimulates an uncontrollable urge to chew as a means of relieving some of the discomfort and as a way to facilitate the removal of their baby teeth.

## Prevention

Knowing this ahead of time, take steps to manage your puppy's environment so he can't inadvertently get himself into trouble. Puppy-proof everything indoors and outdoors. Pick up anything and everything your puppy is likely to seek out and destroy—cushions, magazines, shoes, undergarments,

*The Expert Knows*

### Keep Training Your Puppy

Training your puppy is an ongoing process. You must continue to reinforce positive behaviours and obedience commands—even the easy ones like *sit* and *down*—throughout his entire life. Not only will your puppy grow into an adult dog who enjoys spending time with you, but knowing the basic commands can help prevent problem behaviours before they start. At the very least, you will be better equipped to deal with them should they occur.

electrical cables, cleaning products, medications, garden hoses, and so forth. If you must leave—take your puppy with you or confine him in a crate, exercise pen, or kennel. Do not put your puppy in a position where he can develop bad habits. The point cannot be emphasised enough. Closely supervise your puppy anytime he is not confined. If you leave your puppy unattended or unconfined while you chat on the phone, or take a shower, don't be shocked when you find the heel missing off you favourite pair of shoes.

### Chew Toys

Chew toys, which are available in all shapes, sizes, and flavours, will

Puppy Training and Care

*If you don't want your puppy digging up your tulips, try giving him an area of his own to dig.*

entertain and satisfy your puppy's need to chew for an hour or two, while simultaneously diverting him from chewing on inappropriate items. No scientific method exists for finding the right chew toy. Some are simply better than others. It's really a matter of trial and error and what your puppy prefers. Choose chew toys that are appropriate for the size and chewing style of your puppy. A chew toy designed for a Yorkshire Terrier would be too small for the gnawing and gnashing of a strong-jawed puppy, such as a Rottweiler or Staffordshire Bull Terrier. Avoid toys or bones that are too hard and that may crack your dog's teeth, or those that break apart and present choking hazards.

Remember, puppies are individuals so it is impossible to arbitrarily set an age at which a puppy is through the chewing stage. Some puppies have a stronger desire to chew than others. Much depends on how conscientious and committed you are to managing your puppy's environment, instilling good behaviours, and discouraging unwanted behaviours.

As your puppy grows and matures, his desire to chew will diminish. It is important, however, to continue giving him bones and chew toys throughout his life to exercise his jaw, keep his teeth clean, relieve boredom, release excess energy, and entertain him for a few hours.

## Digging

Dogs love to dig. It's another fact of dog ownership. Some breeds, such as terriers, which were originally bred to hunt vermin in underground dens, dig more than others. Their idea of fun can cause you a significant amount of frustration and heartache—especially when your precious pooch digs right under your prize rose bushes.

## Is He Bored?

Dogs dig for a variety of reason. Some dig holes to bury their favourite bones or toys. Many dogs are attracted to the smell of chicken and cow manure and love to dig and roll in fresh soil and newly fertilised gardens. Others dig to find a cool spot to escape the heat. Many dogs dig out of frustration and boredom. If this is the case with your puppy, use your imagination to come up with fun games that will stimulate his mind, burn energy, and tire him out. For example, take him for a long walk,

## Where to Find a Behaviourist or Trainer

- Breeders and handlers are good starting points. Generally involved in dog sports, they tend to know at least one or two good trainers.
- Ask co-workers, family members, and friends for a referral.
- Check the Association of Pet Dog Trainers (APDT) for names and telephone numbers of training organisations and facilities near you.
- Contact professional organisations, such as the International Association of Animal Behaviour Consultants, or the Association of Pet Behaviour Counsellors.
- Many universities and colleges have animal behaviourists on staff.
- Ask your veterinarian for a referral, since many behaviourists and consultants work with veterinarians.

Some problems, such as aggression and separation anxiety, are difficult and complicated areas of canine behaviour that require expert guidance. If you feel that you and your dog need expert advice, don't hesitate to seek it. You will both be much happier in the long run.

play a game of retrieve, or purchase a food-dispensing puzzle that allows him to exercise his brain as he tries to outsmart the toy. Chew toys that can be stuffed with cheese or peanut butter will provide your puppy with an hour or two of entertainment. Play fun find-it games in which you hide a tasty tidbit of food under a small box or bucket and encourage him to find it. Or play fun hide-and-seek games, in which you encourage him to find you.

### Prevention

A good solution for digging is prevention. Do not allow your puppy free access to garden areas where he can dig and wreak havoc. Install a small fence around the garden, or fence off a section of the garden just for him, where he can dig and dig and dig until his heart's content.

### Jumping Up

Licking faces is a natural behaviour for puppies and adult dogs. If you were to greet your friends' by licking their face, no doubt they would be mortified. Dogs don't operate that way. They see nothing wrong with planting a wet one on your kisser. It's their way of getting close to you and saying, "Hi!" They don't' understand that humans sometimes take offence to what is an otherwise normal canine behaviour.

Of course, for a puppy to lick your face he generally needs to jump on you, which creates all kinds of problems for some humans. If you don't mind your puppy growing into an adult dog who jumps on you and your friends—and some owners don't—then you have nothing to worry about. However, what is cute puppy behaviour today may not be so amusing when he is full grown and has four muddy paws. It is equally unfair to allow him to jump on you but correct him for jumping on visitors, or allow him to jump on you today but not tomorrow when you are wearing clean trousers.

## Prevention

If you do not want your adult dog to jump on you, do not allow the behaviour when he is a puppy. The key is to discourage all occasions of jumping up. Put a lead on your puppy to prevent him from jumping on visitors. This allows you to control his behaviour without grabbing at his fur or collar. When he sits or stands nicely without pawing or mauling your guests, calmly praise, "What a good boy!" and reward him with a tasty tidbit— or a kiss!

You also can prevent jumping by asking your dog to sit for a kiss or biscuit. Of course, it's impossible to expect your puppy to sit until you have thoroughly taught him the *sit* command.

## Running Away

Puppies who grow into adult dogs who run away or refuse to come when they are called cause an enormous amount of angst and frustration for their owners. They can become injured or killed if hit by a car or lost forever. The good news is that this is one of the easiest problems to solve. Seriously!

## Prevention

The key to preventing this problem is to never allow your puppy to be put in a situation in which he is allowed to develop the bad habit of running off. Each and every time you go outside, your puppy should be on lead. It's okay for your puppy to run around and explore his surroundings, but he must do so in an enclosed area, such as a fenced garden, and always have him drag a lead or lightweight long line. When he starts to wander off too far, simply step on the long line and reel him back in with plenty of praise. "There's my silly boy!" Never get in the habit of chasing your puppy or allowing your kids to chase your puppy. Dogs think that this is a fun game, but it teaches

Help Me!

*Jumping up is a natural behaviour for most puppies.*

them to run away from you, which is not only annoying but also dangerous.

Equally important is understanding that your puppy does not come preprogrammed. He has no idea what the word "come" means. You must teach him in a fun and humane manner that "come" means "stop whatever you are doing and run back to me as fast as you can—right now." (See Chapter 6: Train Me!)

## Shyness/Fearfulness

How shy a puppy is depends partly on his genetic makeup. Remember those inherited behaviours discussed in Chapter 6? If your puppy's parents—particularly his mother—were shy or spooky, he most likely inherited this trait, too. Or, at the very least, he's inherited a predisposition to be afraid of unfamiliar people, spaces, sights, sounds, and so forth. Some breeds are more sensitive than others, and they tend to be more shy, too. However, puppies are first and foremost individuals, and this is why littermates raised under the same conditions will develop differently.

Whatever your puppy's background or genetic makeup, you must be aware of his shyness. Pay attention to how he encounters strange noises, sights, and situations. Does he show signs of anxiety or a high level of insecurity and fearfulness in general? Does he run to meet new people or try to avoid them by shying or running away? Does he move away from or toward an object or person? Does he show alarm or panic at new sounds or strange objects?

Socialisation is a key factor in raising a well-adjusted adult dog and doubly important if you own a shy or fearful puppy. To maximise your puppy's future—especially a shy puppy—you must invest a lot of time socialising him. Begin as soon as possible by exposing him in a fun and safe environment to all the sights and sounds he is likely to encounter as an adult dogs. (See Chapter 6 for how to socialise a puppy.) A dog is never too old to socialise. However, habits become ingrained, and it becomes progressively more difficult to manage his shyness or fearfulness as he grows older. With diligence, common sense, and a bit of luck, your puppy will hopefully begin to relax and enjoy the company of other dogs and people, as well as outings to the park, beach, or a walk around the block.

*Talk to your vet if you notice a change in your puppy's behaviour.*

**FAMILY-FRIENDLY TIP**

## What Children Should Know about Dogs

Raising kids can be a challenge—even on the best of days! Throw a new puppy into the mix, and you've got your hands full. Kids and dogs seem to naturally go together, but keeping both dogs and kids safe takes a well-thought-out game plan. Children should learn:

- That not all dogs are as friendly as their own. Always ask the owner for permission before petting a strange dog.
- To offer their hand with their palm facing up (like feeding sugar cubes to a horse).
- To approach dogs from the side and pet them under their chin, on the side of the face, or on chest. Avoid petting a dog's head. Many dogs don't like this behaviour and will shy away or possibly nip.

- To never go into a house or garden where a dog is present unless the owners are in attendance.
- To stay away from chained, fenced, or stray dogs.
- To always get help from an adult when dealing with an injured dog, because they are more likely to bite as a reflex to the pain.
- To never stare directly at a dog. The dog may perceive this as a challenge.
- To never kick, hit, pinch, yell, tease, or taunt any dog in the name of fun and games.
- To let sleeping dogs lie. Do not disturb dogs who are eating, sleeping, or chewing on something.

# Chapter 8

# Play With Me!

Puppies are never too young to begin training, playing, and learning fun games. That said, dogs under the age of two should never be allowed to jump because too much pressure on developing joints can injure your puppy and lead to lifelong problems, and no one wants that.

**P**uppies are smart and energetic and, in the absence of adequate physical and mental stimulation, puppies (and adult dogs) will find their own ways to stimulate their brains, burn excess energy, and alleviate frustrations. This is when behavioural problems generally arise. Basic training for the following competitive events and programmes could be perfect for your puppy, and help strengthen the bond between the two of you.

## Competitive Events

Most organisations sanctioning events do not allow puppies under six months of age to be on the show grounds, let alone compete. That said, it is never too early to begin instilling behaviours that will help your puppy grow into an adult dog who enjoys and excels in competitive venues.

National clubs and registries, such as the Kennel Club (KC) and your local breed club, offer a wide variety of activities in which your dog can compete. Finding the perfect sport or pastime for you and your puppy is relatively easy because, after all, there are countless activities from which to choose. You may have to try a few different activities, but chances are there is a canine sport—or two!— with your puppy's name on it. Let's take a look at a few of the more popular events.

## Agility

Agility is one of the fastest growing sports for dogs, and one of the most exciting, fast-paced canine sports for spectators. It is an extension of obedience but without all the formality and precision. Agility courses are more reminiscent of equestrian courses that include assorted jumps and hurdles. In agility, dogs demonstrate their agile nature and versatility by manoeuvring through a timed obstacle course of jumps, tunnels, A-frames, weave poles, see-saws, ramps, and a pause box. Unlike the higher levels of obedience, agility handlers are permitted to talk to their dogs, and even to give multiple commands.

There are a number of different levels of agility competition. Dogs progress from starters level, to novice, intermediate and advanced level. At each level, the courses are tougher, with increasingly difficult handling points.

The challenge of agility is to be able to control your

*Often, you can teach a puppy a trick by capturing his natural behaviour.*

dog in a wide-open area, and direct him to go where you want. It looks easy enough, but courses are set with twists, turns and sometimes with deliberate traps, which can tempt your dog to take the wrong course. If a dog takes the wrong course he is eliminated. He loses points for refusals, knocked poles, and missed contact points. The winner is the dog who completes a clear round in the fastest time.

Agility events in the UK are run under Kennel Club rules, and dogs are not allowed to compete until they are eighteen months old. This is a safeguard to protect bones and joints, which are vulnerable while a dog is still growing.

Even if you do not want to reach competitive level, you and your Puppy can still enjoy agility as a fun, non-competitive pastime. Most training organisations have classes for beginners. You will need good basic obedience such as a solid "down", "wait" and "come" before you are ready to even start thinking about taking up agility at a fun level.

The number one consideration in an agility class is safety. This is one of the few sports that can result in serious injuries. Falling off an A-frame or dog walk can break bones. Neglecting to warm up before jumping can cause serious muscle injuries. Out-of-control dogs that are off-lead can also hurt other dogs.

Before you sign up for a class, visit one in action. Does the trainer emphasise safety? Are the larger dogs under control? If the answers are "yes" sign up! You and your Puppy will have

## Sports and Safety

Safety must always come first in any activity, especially fast-paced, high-energy activities like agility and canine freestyle. Before beginning any physically challenging activity, have your puppy examined by a veterinarian to rule out any joint or other medical issues. Here are some additional ways to keep your puppy safe:

- Always check with your vet before jumping young puppies. Too much pressure on developing joints can injure your puppy and lead to lifelong problems, and no one wants that.

- Low-stress activities are wonderful for puppies, such as fun tug games, chase recalls, hide-and-seek, and so forth.

- When the weather is hot, confine your sports and games to the early morning or evening hours to prevent heat-related illnesses.

- Always monitor your puppy for signs of fatigue and stress.

- Have plenty of water available, especially on hot days.

a great time together. If you want to start in agility with your dog your first port of call should be a local agility club, ring the secretary or instructor there and discuss your dog, the level of training you currently have and any health or fitness problems that your dog may suffer–agility is a physically demanding spot even at a fun level. Ask if you can come to watch the training and talk to people with experience, you may be invited to take your dog down so that he can be assessed for fitness and obedience. To find a local agility club in your area, contact the Kennel Club www.thekennelclub. org.uk or our national breed club. If you know other dog owners who take part in agility, word of mouth recommendation is also a great place to start, although you should always check the trainer or club's credentials yourself.

### Getting Started

Most organisations have age limits in place to prevent dogs from competing in sanctioned events before they are physically and mentally mature. The KC do not allow dogs to enter an agility ring until they are fifteen months old.

If necessary, consult your veterinarian and carefully consider at what age it is safe for your puppy to begin training—especially jumping, weave poles, A-frames, and so forth.

To successfully compete in agility, your dog will need basic obedience skills, and it is never too early to begin instilling those behaviours. Many handling skills and behaviours are specific to agility, such as teaching your puppy to take direction from both your right and left side, and while running away from you; turning left and right after a jump; targeting for contact training, and so forth. Ideally, you should spend your puppy's formative first year teaching the ground work. If you have all that in place at one year of age, the equipment training goes very quickly. That said, it behooves you to train with someone who is experienced in teaching and

*You can start your puppy on groundwork if he's too young to jump.*

competing in agility. Otherwise, handling and training problems are likely to develop, and these are often difficult to backtrack and correct.

*The Good Citizen Scheme programme rewards dogs with good manners..*

### Good Citizen Scheme (GCS)

Training and interacting with your puppy is always fun, but if organised competitions aren't your cup of tea, the KC's Good Citizen Scheme (GCS) might be the perfect alternative. The GCS programme rewards dogs who exhibit good manners, and what's more impressive than a well-mannered puppy who grows into a well-behaved adult dog? This is particularly important for breeds that have acquired, albeit undeservedly, bad-boy images. The noncompetitive test evaluates your dog's behaviour in practical situations at home, in public, and in the presence of unfamiliar people and other dogs. The pass/no-pass test is designed to measure a dog's reactions to distractions, friendly strangers, and supervised isolation. Additionally, the dog must sit politely while being petted, walk on a loose lead, walk through a crowd, and respond to basic obedience commands.

Breed clubs, trainers, and rescue centres usually have information on GCS training and testing programmes. Many CGC graduates go on to obedience, therapy work, or other canine sports. Although there is no age requirement, dogs must be old enough to have received their immunisations.

### Canine Freestyle

Canine freestyle allows you and your dog to kick up your heels, so to speak. Patterned after Olympic skating, Canine Freestyle is a choreographed performance between a dog and handler, set to music. It can include twists, turns, leg kicks, pivots, and other cool and creative manoeuvres. Advanced competitors teach their dog to crawl, back up, wave, bow, side-step, bounce, roll over, and so forth. The World Canine Freestyle Organisation (WCFO) holds competitions throughout the country, and titles are awarded to high scores in technical merit and artistic impression.

## Getting Started

Dogs must be six months of age to compete in WCFO competitions. As with most canine events, canine freestyle requires a strong and mutually respectful human–canine relationship. Therefore, you will want to start immediately instilling basic obedience commands, such as sit, down, stand, and come, and teaching fun tricks and moves, such as spins, pivots, jumps, and so forth. Again, this is a lot for a young puppy to learn, and most dogs are twelve to eighteen months old before they can physically and mentally perform many of the manoeuvres in a competitive environment. Look for obedience trainers who compete in canine freestyle and can guide you through the rules and regulations as well.

## Dog Shows (Conformation)

Conformation shows are the signature event of the competitive dog world, and your puppy may have the goods to be a champion. Before you post your entry form and fees, let's take a look at how they work and what you will need to know.

For the newcomer, it often appears as if the dogs are competing against one another. And, in a sense, they are. However, the judge is not comparing the quality of one dog against the quality of another dog, but rather evaluating how closely each dog measures up to the ideal dog as outlined in that particular breed's breed standard. The dog who comes closest, in the judge's opinion, is the winner.

The best way to understand the conformation ring is to think of it in terms of an elimination process. Classes are divided by sex, with males and females being judged separately within their breed. Male dogs are always judged first and, after being placed first through fourth, the females go through the same judging process. After the regular classes have been judged, the first-place winners of each class compete for Winners Dog and Winners Bitch. Again, males and females are judged separately, and the best male and best female receive championship points. They then compete for Best of Breed. The Best of Breed

*To be a show dog, your puppy must learn to "stand for examination" in order to be judged.*

winner then goes on to the Group competition, and from there, moves to on to compete for the coveted and most prestigious award: Best in Show.

To get started in conformation competitions, the best thing to do is attend a number of dog shows. Most handlers love talking shop, and they are more than happy to answer questions, provided, of course, they are not busy grooming or getting ready to go into the ring.

## Getting Started

The KC requires dogs to be six months of age at the time of competition.

Before sending in your entry forms, your dog should be well versed in breed-ring etiquette—meaning he should accept being examined head to toe, gait on lead (move at a trot), and stack (stand or pose) freely. He should be well socialised with other dogs and people, of sound temperament, physically fit and conditioned, bathed, and groomed according to the breed's standard. Many trainers and breeders offer handling classes that can help you and your dog prepare for an exciting career in the breed ring.

## Obedience Trials

Obedience trials go well beyond the Good Citizen Scheme requirements and, if you love training your dog, obedience competitions may be your cup of tea. Obedience trials require your dog to perform a number of specific exercises that showcase his training and how well he obeys your

## Service Opportunities

Did you know that your well-mannered puppy can make a wonderful therapy dog who provides unconditional love, companionship, and emotional support to nursing home, hospital, assisted-living, and mental-health residents? Owners volunteering with their dogs' make regularly scheduled visits and brighten the lives of residents by providing stimulation, companionship, and a vehicle for conversation and interaction. Puppies and adult dogs must be well-mannered and have a sound temperament. While not a requirement, it does help if your dog is certified for therapy work and, at the minimum, obedience trained and in possession of a CGC certificate.

Many local and national organisations—some associated with hospitals, rescue centres, and other institutions—can help you and your puppy get started in therapy work. Pets As Therapy (PAT) regulates, evaluates, tests, and registers therapy dogs.

commands. Dogs can compete at several different levels: Pre-beginners, Beginners, Novice, Class A, Class B and Class C, with each level being increasingly more difficult.

### Getting Started

Dogs must be six months old before entering an KC-sanctioned obedience competition.

*If your puppy responds well to learning basic commands, he might be on his way to becoming a great obedience competitor.*

That said, most dogs are not physically or mentally mature enough to compete at six months. Lots and lots of work goes into training an obedience dog to perform specific commands in a stressful and competitive environment. Entering your dog before he is physically and mentally ready can do untold damage to a dog's confidence and eagerness to perform in the future. Generally speaking, most dogs are not ready for the pre-beginners obedience ring until they are eighteen to twenty-four months of age or older.

Ideally, you should find a trainer who teaches and competes in obedience competitions, because many of the methods for teaching competition obedience differ from basic pet obedience. Equally important, he can show you how to instil all the behaviours your puppy will need to grow into a confident, fun, obedience dog.

### Rally Obedience

Rally obedience, although very popular in the United States, has yet to be sanctioned by the Kennel Club in the UK. It was created with the average dog owner in mind. Less formal and rigorous than traditional obedience trials, dog and handler proceed at their own pace through a course of designated stations. Each station has a

sign providing instructions regarding the skill that is to be performed, such as Halt & Sit, Right Turn, About Right Turn, and so forth.

Dogs and handlers can compete in three levels: Novice, Advanced, and Excellent. Like traditional obedience, each level becomes increasingly more demanding, and dogs and handlers must receive three qualifying scores in each level before progressing to the next level. Dogs who earn at least 70 points out of a possible 100 are awarded a leg. Three legs are required for a Rally obedience title.

### Tracking

Designed to test a dog's ability to recognise and track a human scent over varying terrains and climatic changes, you can teach your dog to track for fun, such as finding his toys or a treat that you have hidden in the house or garden, or you can teach him to track as a sport. Although in America, tracking is a discipline in its own right, here in the UK it forms part of Working Trials. Dogs must progress through levels of increasing difficulty known as "stakes". The stakes are: Companion Dog (CD), Utility Dog (UD), Working Dog (WD), Tracking Dog (TD), and Patrol Dog (PD). Each stake is comprised of three sections: nosework, agility and control. Nosework tests the dog's ability to follow a scent trail.

## Travel

Puppies love a good road trip and while most are quite adaptable and make wonderful travellers—don't wait until you are on the road to discover yours is not! Ideally, it is best to accustom your puppy to travelling while he is young and receptive to new adventures. If you have any older puppy, say, six to eight months old, don't despair. With a bit of patience, he too can learn to love road trips, be they across town or across the country.

## Around Town

Weather permitting, your puppy is sure to enjoy short trips to the market, bank, and so forth. Your puppy should ride in his crate to curtail any vomiting or potty accidents, and to prevent him from distracting you, gnawing on the leather seats, eating your mobile phone, or ransacking the groceries. If you should stop suddenly or get in an accident, your puppy will be safer if confined in his crate. He should also be wearing his buckle collar with ID tag. If your errands take you away from home for more than an hour or so, be sure

## The Expert Knows

### When Hot Is Too Hot

Going places with your puppy is always fun, be it around town or across the country, but plan ahead during hot weather. On an 85°F (29°C) day, the temperature in a parked car, even with the all the windows partly open, can quickly reach 120°F (49°C). Your puppy can suffer serious brain damage or death in the time it takes you to make a quick trip into the grocery shop or bank. Never leave your puppy unattended in the car.

to carry bottled water in case he gets thirsty and paper bags for cleaning up after him should a pit stop be necessary.

## Longer Car Rides

Longer trips require a bit more planning, but they can be equally pleasurable for both you and your dog. If your puppy is used to riding in the car, longer trips should not present too many problems. Travelling with a dog is a lot like travelling with children. You will need to stop every few hours to let your puppy relieve himself and burn off pent-up energy. Unless your puppy is a seasoned traveller, it is best to limit his food intake two hours before travelling. Feed the bulk of his food after you have stopped for the day. Talk to your veterinarian about any additional vaccinations or medications your puppy might need, depending on your destination.

## Flying the Friendly Skies

Airplane journeys require quite a bit more planning, but they are well worth the effort if your puppy enjoys being with you. With the advent of the Pets Passport Scheme travelling abroad wth your puppy is much easier. Not all airlines accept dogs, and many limit the number of dogs accepted on each flight, so planning ahead is essential. Your puppy will need specific types of documentation, including a health certificate issued by a veterinarian within ten days of travelling. Check before travelling to any other country, their quarantine regulations. Notify the airlines that your puppy is travelling with you. Puppies and pint-sized dogs can ride in the cabin, but your puppy may be required to travel in the cargo hold area, depending on his size. Therefore, when scheduling flights, try to book nonstop flights during the middle of the week, avoiding holiday or weekend travel. Avoid layovers and plane changes, if possible. During warm weather, choose flights early in the morning or late in the evening; in cooler months, choose midday flights.

## Accommodation

If your travels with your puppy include staying at a hotel, or campground, call ahead to be sure they accept dogs. Not everyone accepts dogs—even a well-behaved puppy. Some facilities allow dogs in the rooms, but may require that the dog be crated. Some larger hotels provide kennel facilities. Many require a refundable pet deposit or nonrefundable pet fee.

## Packing for Puppy

When travelling, your puppy will need his own travel bag of necessities. In addition to his crate, collar, and lead, be sure to pack these must-have items:

- Enough food and bottled water to last for the journey—and perhaps a day or two longer in case of unexpected delays.
- Current health certificate and passport if travelling abroad

*Using his nose to track a scent may come naturally to your pup.*

- Current photographs, to be used for ID should he become lost.
- Pooper-scooper, paper towels, or plastic bags for picking up after your dog.
- First-aid kit and any medications and prescriptions, if necessary.
- Chew toys, bones, tug toys, balls, and the like.
- A favourite blanket or bed.
- An adequate supply of doggie towels for quick cleanups, in the event your dog gets wet, dirty, or injured.

Puppies are adaptable, and most likely yours won't care where you go or what you do as long as he's included in your plans and he can spend time with you.

# FAMILY-FRIENDLY TIP

## Travelling with Puppies and Kids

Puppies make excellent travelling companions, and travelling with them is similar to travelling with toddlers and small children. Make frequent pit stops a priority so that your puppy can relieve himself, stretch his legs, and burn off some pent-up energy. Incorporate your children by having them keep track of the sun so it isn't beating through the window on him, causing him to overheat. Let them track scheduled breaks and sound the alarm when it's time for a pit stop. Older children can help clean up any messes and make sure he gets enough water. Travelling with your four-legged friend takes planning and a good deal of patience but, with a bit of organisation, there's no reason your precious pooch can't come along, too.

Play With Me!

# Resources

## Associations and Organisations

### Breed Clubs

**American Kennel Club (AKC)**
5580 Centerview Drive
Raleigh, NC 27606
Telephone: (919) 233-9767
Fax: (919) 233-3627
E-mail: info@akc.org
www.akc.org

**Canadian Kennel Club (CKC)**
89 Skyway Avenue, Suite 100
Etobicoke, Ontario M9W 6R4
Telephone: (416) 675-5511
Fax: (416) 675-6506
E-mail: information@ckc.ca
www.ckc.ca

**Federation Cynologique Internationale (FCI)**
Secretariat General de la FCI
Place Albert 1er, 13
B – 6530 Thuin
Belqique
www.fci.be

**The Kennel Club**
1 Clarges Street
London
W1J 8AB
Telephone: 0870 606 6750
Fax: 0207 518 1058
www.the-kennel-club.org.uk

**United Kennel Club (UKC)**
100 E. Kilgore Road
Kalamazoo, MI 49002-5584
Telephone: (269) 343-9020
Fax: (269) 343-7037
E-mail: pbickell@ukcdogs.com
www.ukcdogs.com

## Pet Sitters

**National Association of Registered Petsitters**
www.dogsit.com

**UK Petsitters**
www.ukpetsitter.com

## Rescue Organisations and Animal Welfare Groups

**British Veterinary Association Animal Welfare Foundation**
7 Mansfield Street
London W1G 9NQ
Telephone: 0207 436 2970
Email: bva-awf@bva.co.uk
www.bva-awf.org.uk

**Dogs Trust**
17 Wakley Street
London
EC1V 7RQ
Telephone: 0207 837 0006
www.dogstrust.org.uk

**Royal Society for the Prevention of Cruelty to Animals (RSPCA)**
Telephone: 0870 3335 999
Fax: 0870 7530 284
www.rspca.org.uk

**Scottish Society for the Prevention of Cruelty to Animals (SSPCA)**
Braehead Mains, 603
Queensferry Road
Edinburgh EH4 6EA
Telephone: 0131 339 4777
Email: enquiries@scottishspca.org
www.scottishspca.org

## Therapy

**Pets As Therapy**
3a Grange Farm Cottages
Wycombe Road
Saunderton
Princes Risborough
Bucks  HP27 9NS
www.petsastherapy.org

## Training

**Association of Pet Dog Trainers (APDT)**
PO Box 17
Kampsford GL7 4W7
Telephone: 01285 810 811

**Association of Pet Behaviour Counsellors**
PO Box 46
Worcester WR8 9YS
Telephone: 01386 750743
Email:: info@apbc.org.uk
www.apbc.org.uk

**British Institute of Professional Dog Trainers**
www.bipdt.net

# Veterinary and Health Resources

**British Veterinary Association (BVA)**
7 Mansfield Street
London
W1G 9NQ
Telephone: 020 7636 6541
Fax: 020 7436 2970
E-mail: bvahq@bva.co.uk
www.bva.co.uk

**British Veterinary Hospitals Association (BHVA)**
Station Bungalow
Main Road, Stockfield
Northumberland NE43 7HJ
Telephone: 07966 901619
www.BVHA.org.uk

**Royal College of Veterinary Surgeons (RCVS)**
Belgravia House
62-64 Horseferry Road
London SW1P 2AF
Telephone: 0207 222 2001
www.rcvs.org.uk

**Association of Chartered Physiotherapists Specialising in Animal Therapy (ACPAT)**
52 Littleham Road
Exmouth, Devon EX8 2QJ
Telephone: 01395 270648
www.acpat.org.uk

**Association of British Veterinary Acupuncturists (ABVA)**
66A Easthorpe, Southwell
Nottinghamshire NG25 0HZ
www.abva.co.uk

# Index

Note: **Boldfaced** numbers
indicate illustrations.

**111**

Index

## About the Author

Tracy Libby is an award-winning freelance writer and co-author of *Building Blocks for Performance* (Alpine 2002), and several breed books for the Terra-Nova series and Animal Planet® Pet Care Library. Her articles have appeared in numerous publications, including the AKC *Gazette*, *Puppies USA*, *You and Your Dog*, and Dog Fancy's *Popular Dogs* series. She is a member of the Dog Writers Association of America and a recipient of the Ellsworth S. Howell award for distinguished dog writing. She lives in Oregon, and has been involved in the sport of dogs for 20 years, exhibiting in conformation and obedience.

## Photo Credits

Angela kay Agnew (Shutterstock): 101; Lars Christensen (Shutterstock): 63; Condor 36 (Shutterstock): 67; Perry Correll (Shutterstock): 94; Waldemar Dabrowski (Shutterstock): 19, 71, 88; Tad Denson (Shutterstock): 93; Jaimie Duplass (Shutterstock): 50; Amparo Fontanet (Shutterstock): 86; Isabelle Francais: 10, 16, 20, 26, 29, 30, 32, 34, 41, 42, 44, 45, 46, 47, 52, 77, 80, 81, 82, 102, 106; Naomi Hasegawa (Shutterstock): 68; Kato Inowe (Shutterstock): 55; Eric Isselee (Shutterstock): 3, 12, 18, 40 (right), 58, 69, 72, 74; Mary Ann Kahn: 40 (left); Bianca Lagalla: 9; Erik Lam (Shutterstock): 98; Jim Larson (Shutterstock): 91; Mircea Maieru (Shutterstock): 48; Shirelle Reggio Manning: 6; Sean Nel (Shutterstock): 14; Ellen Perlson: 100; Pieter (Shutterstock): 13, 27, 28, 43, 54, 60, 63, 73, 79, 89, 92, 99, 109; Rick's Photography (Shutterstock): 24; Rix Pix (Shutterstock): 104; Shutterstock: 11, 36, 38, 57, 66, 75; SueC (Shutterstock): 64; Mariusz Szachowski (Shutterstock): 56; Ferenc Szelepcsenyi (Shutterstock): 78; Albert H. Teich (Shutterstock): 84; verityjohnson (Shutterstock): 96; Lopatinsky Vladislav (Shutterstock): 61; Wojciech Zbieg (Shutterstock): 95;

Cover photo: Adrian Moisei (Shutterstock)